To my Friend Russ,
Thank you for your
Service To our count
God Bless
John T Senka

Wounded Body – Healing Spirit

An Arkport Soldier's Inspirational Journey
As a Vietnam Combat Veteran

by
John T. Senka

Post-Traumatic Stress Disorder

Acute Clinical Depression

Wounded Body – Healing Spirit
An Arkport Soldier's Inspirational Journey
As a Vietnam Combat Veteran

by

John T. Senka

First Edition Copyright 2004

Copyright in the United States of America under all International
and Pan-American Copyright Conventions.

All rights reserved. No part of this publication may be reproduced or
utilized in any form or by any means, electronic, mechanical,
photocopying, recording, or by any informational storage and retrieval
system, without the written permission of the Author, except for a
reviewer who may quote brief passages in a review.

Published by

Brundage Publishing
Room 203 Executive Office Building
33 West State Street
Binghamton, NY 13901

Jacket design by Amanda Nord

Library of Congress
Control Number: 2004104028

ISBN Number: 1-892451-18-2

Printed in the United States of America

**DEDICATION**

To my wife Sandy, were it not for your encouragement, your reassurance, your loyalty and your love, I would have given up hope. Living with me and for me has not been easy. "Thank You" and "I Love You" are not enough. To my God, Thank you for not abandoning me.

"FREEDOM ISN'T FREE"
It is the soldier, not the reporter, who has given us
freedom of the press.
It is the soldier, not the poet, who has given us
freedom of speech.
It is the soldier, not the campus organizer, who
has
given us the freedom to demonstrate.
It is the soldier, not the lawyer, who has given us
the right to a fair trial.
It is the soldier who salutes the flag,
serves under the flag,
and whose coffin is draped by the flag.

MEMORIAM DEDICATION

To my buddies who died in Vietnam

PFC. Henry Maul
Spec. 4 Justin Anderson
PFC. Phil Glenn
PFC. Malcolm True
Sgt. Jay Schmid
Spec. 4 David Briggs
LCPL Freddy Kemp
LCPL Joe Barillo

To

My parents Joe and Julia Katsur and John Senka

And to

My best friends Paul C. "Wink" Wolfgruber
John R. "Bud" Hubric

"To live in the hearts of those we love is not to die"

ACKNOWLEDGEMENTS

This is my first attempt at writing a book. The idea was conceived during my darkest hour. I was battling Post-Traumatic Stress Disorder from my combat in Vietnam and Acute Clinical Depression at the same time. Writing a book, particularly an autobiography, is like baring one's soul; it is like standing naked in the Village Square. My purpose in writing this book is an effort to help others deal with their problems and challenges by learning from my experiences in dealing with Post-Traumatic Stress Disorder and Acute Clinical Depression.

I owe a debt of gratitude to my wife Sandy; my daughter and son-in-law Debbie and Don; my son and daughter-in-law, Johnny and Tambi; my son Jeff and his life partner, Stan; my co-workers Emily, Challiss, and Anne; to my caring friends Jay, Chuck, Bev, Dorenda, Greg, Al, Connie, Ron, Donita, Bill, Carol, Ralph, Penny, Lee, Luanne; my in-laws Louie and Florence; Rita; the students at the San Xavier Mission School; Father Austin; Dr. Fass, Tony, Dr. Quirion, Vince, Joe, Kim, Dave, Nancy, Bob, Bonnie, Dick, Ellie; and many other friends in my caring community.

Special thanks to my friend, Challiss Wolcott, for typing my manuscripts, and to the Brundage Publishing staff who worked on my book: Barrie Hoople, David Ortiz, Tiffany Denepitiya, and Frank Resseguie.

Table of Contents

Chapter		*Page*

DARK NIGHT OF THE SOUL

November of 1999 was not just the end of the century, but the beginning of weeks of pain and agony for me. It was in that month of my life that I fell into a deep dark hole, my own private hell on earth. My psychologists and psychiatrists feared that I wouldn't be able to climb out of it.

It was a shock to all that knew me. As one of my colleagues, John Chrisman described me, "Senka, you are one of the toughest sons of bitches I know."   It was true for the most part; I had always been able to handle whatever life threw at me. I never backed down from a challenge or fight of any kind. I had overcome plenty of obstacles in my life and was proud of who I was, but **now** when I looked in the mirror, I saw a stranger. I no longer knew who I was. I was afraid of everything. My spirit was broken. Just getting out of bed was a major accomplishment. It was easier to lay in bed in the fetal position. I prayed each night that I wouldn't wake up the next morning. I had entered the "Dark Night of the Soul."

Before I explain what the Dark Night of the Soul was for me, I think that it is important to know who I am and where I come from. I believe that a single experience can't cause a human being to go from a strong, happy, functioning individual to a scared animal ready to end a miserable existence, but for me it was an accumulation of a lifetime of experiences.

This book is about the chain of events that lead to my Dark Night of the Soul and to my escape from it.

Chapter 1

FAMILY THREADS

My grandfather from my Mother's side, Mike Jurkovic, was killed in combat during World War I. Mike was an infantryman in the Czechoslovakian Army and left behind a wife and three young daughters, one of which was to become my Mother. Ironically, he was buried in Luck, Russia. I always wondered if fate performed a kindness for him since he was never alive long enough to deal with the mental aftereffects of war.

My other grandfather, Grandpa Senka, also served in World War I and was wounded; he suffered from what we now know as Post-Traumatic Stress Disorder. He spent much of his time in Veteran's Hospitals, and much of his time self-medicating with whiskey. He made life miserable for his wife and seven children. As a young man newly married, he and his new wife Katherine moved from Czechoslovakia to Michigan expecting to find the streets paved in gold. My Father, the oldest of the seven Senka children, was born in Michigan but returned to Europe with his family when he was an infant. Apparently Grandpa Senka missed friends and family, or perhaps the streets weren't as gold plated as he had envisioned.

My Father had a hard life growing up in Czechoslovakia. He and his brothers were constantly involved in physical confrontations with Grandpa Senka who constantly drank. Grandpa Senka owned a bar, a bowling alley, and a nice home. Unfortunately fate wasn't in his favor during his life, especially when he lost everything in a poker game. His wife and children were forced to move out of a nice house that they had come to love and appreciate.

As a result, the brothers became tough; Uncle Simone became the champion boxer of Czechoslovakia and in 1953 went to Madrid, Spain to win the Welterweight Championship of all Europe. During the Great Depression, which was considerably worse in Europe than in the United States, my Father and his friends would sneak into Austria to buy pepper to sell back in their own country on the black market. In addition, they had a reputation as poachers, shooting wild game out of season in order to eat and survive. When he was in his early twenties, he was drafted into the Slovak Army and served honorably. In the late 1930's, he finally fulfilled his dream of leaving Europe to return to America.

He settled in a Slovak neighborhood in New Jersey, found work, and enjoyed bachelorhood. He had the classic immigrant dream of some day having a family, his own business, and giving his children the life he never had. His greatest regret was his lack of a formal education.

He eventually met my Mother, a shy Slovak girl, who knew him only by name and reputation in her hometown of Gajary. She had convinced her family to allow her to visit America for the 1939 World's Fair. Her ship was the last to leave Germany before Hitler stopped all travel. She had no idea that World War II would breakout and it would be thirty years before she would see her family again.

Julia Jurkovic and John Senka were married, and like all newlyweds expected to live happily ever after.

Father John and Mother Julia, wedding picture

Unfortunately for the second time in my Mother's life, she was affected by war when her new husband, only a few years out of the Slovak Army, was now drafted and sent to serve in the Pacific with the United States Navy.

It was hard for her being alone in a strange country. She found work in factories and worked as a nanny to the children of affluent Jewish families in the New York City area. In 1944, my Mother gave birth to a son named John, who sadly died after living only three days. She nearly died during the process and was told she would not be able to have more children. However in 1945, she gave birth to my sister Jean while my father was away serving in the Pacific.

After the war, John returned to his wife and daughter in New Jersey. Although suffering from "war incurred maladies," my Father chose to take his discharge and move on with his life and with his dreams.

In 1947, my Mother was pregnant with me. The family of three would soon have a new addition. They hoped for a son.

The morning of June 27, 1947, my Father said goodbye to his wife and daughter and departed for his job at Spencer-

Kellogg. When he stepped onto the sidewalk in front of his apartment building, he collapsed. He was rushed to Bergen County Hospital where he remained in a coma. As my Mother spoke to him, she told him how much she needed him as tears rolled down his face. Two days later at the age of thirty-five, my Dad died never having the opportunity to meet his son who was born ten days after his death. Tragedy, it seemed, was firmly embedded in my family's destiny from early on before my own existence in this world.

Chapter 2

SHARING FRIENDS AND SIBLING WARS

I was born July 12, 1947, and was named John after my Father. My Mother now faced the hardest ordeal: She was young, had no family in this country, spoke little English, and now had two young children to care for. We didn't have any money and my Father's GI Insurance was worthless since it lapsed.

My Mother worked and lived her life solely for the purpose of her children. In those days, people took care of themselves or helped one another. They didn't depend on the government to take care of them. She wore black for two years after my Father died as part of her mourning, but still my Mom was tough and determined. As much as she missed my Father, she decided that if the right man ever came along, she would remarry and give her kids a better life.

In 1950, Joe Katsur, a potato farmer from Upstate New York was going to New York City for New Year's Eve. A blizzard stranded him at the home of Steve and Rose Hluchan who told him about their friend, Julie Senka. Rose called my Mother and encouraged her to celebrate New Year's Eve with her, her husband, and Joe. Joe was a bachelor and forty years old. He was a good man who was not deterred by the fact that my Mom came with a ready-made family. After a long distance romance, they fell in love and were married. We moved to Arkport, a small village in Upstate New York. My sister and I were thrilled to have grass, fruit trees, and a garden. It was such a difference from the apartment house in Gutenburg, New Jersey.

Step Dad, Mom, John, and sister Jean

Although our potato farms encompassed more than 600 acres, we lived in the village twelve miles from the farms. When I was about three or four years old, I met Chuck, Duffy, Ron, Wink, Bernie, and Jay. They were neighborhood youngsters, some of whom are still my closest friends. The 1950s were years of innocence. Everyone knew one another and looked out for each other in the community. People sat on their front porches. It wasn't uncommon to see children and adults playing croquet, hopscotch, charades, and other games together.

In grade school, I was a good student and enjoyed taking part in school choral programs. In kindergarten, I sang "Take Me Out to the Ball Game," and in 2nd or 3rd grade, I belted out "Yellow Rose of Texas" for the audience. In retrospect, I know I didn't have the talent I thought I had, but I'm sure I was entertaining and provided folks with a good laugh. Like most youngsters living in the '50s, our favorite pastime was baseball. We organized our own teams and played constantly from morning 'til dark and every boy's bicycle had a leather baseball glove hanging from the handlebars.

The people were friendly and caring. We always found plenty to do, whether it was hiking the hills and forests, catching minnows in the creek, fishing at the dam, organizing a neighborhood circus, or starting a lemonade business. As we grew older, we got involved in scouting, Little League, and swimming at the dam. Most boys got brush cuts as soon as school recessed for the summer. We'd either go barefoot or wear black high top sneakers. Bicycles took us where we needed to go and as we got older, we would hitchhike to Hornell, the nearest city. It was safe in those days; most of the cars that picked us up were residents of our village.

In 1952, my brother Joey was born and in 1956 another brother, Bobby, was born. The relationship with my sister Jean was strained to say the least. Being two years older than me, she had always been able to control me. She had a sharp tongue and wouldn't hesitate to point out my physical defects such as being too short for my age, extremely skinny, having ears that were too large for my head, or that my two front teeth stuck out. Looking back, I now realize she had very low self-esteem. She had few friends, whereas I was liked in the community and had many friends.

I remember clearly the time she and I got into a verbal confrontation that eventually became physical. Since she was taller and heavier than I was, I had never dared fight her. One particular day, however, I had enough, and viciously attacked her by pulling her hair and slamming her to the floor. My Mother tried to stop it, but my Dad, in all his infinite wisdom, told her to stay out of it. I think my Dad had seen the abuse I had taken from Jean since I was little and decided it was payback time. My sister was so upset about the beating she had just received from her skinny little brother that she took my Mother's good kitchen radio and smashed it into hundreds of pieces on the kitchen floor. Our relationship was never the same; I swore I'd never take her abuse again. Unfortunately this was just the beginning of a miserable brother-sister relationship that would span several decades.

As a child, I had a great time living in Arkport. We lived on Main Street where there was always something going on. Chuck, Ron, Duffy and Bernie lived within a stone's throw. We all rode bicycles, and spent our time either playing baseball, fishing, or building forts in the woods. Kids back then hung out in their own neighborhoods, but would often challenge similar gangs in other neighborhoods to a baseball or touch football game. Everyone in town knew one another. We got along pretty well except for the occasional verbal confrontation that would escalate into a fistfight. We all took a thump now and then, but eventually learned to get along.

I recall that on May Day (May 1st), we would make baskets out of wallpaper scraps and fill them with spring flowers that we had picked. We would then hang them on our neighbors' doors, ring the bell and run and hide. It would give us such pleasure to see one of the neighborhood ladies find their gift. Life was simple then. People did more together back then. TV was new and personal computers were not invented. Porches were built on the front of homes so you could see your neighbors. Today we have no porches, but only secluded decks on the rear of our houses.

When school closed for the summer, our mom's would send us to Bing's Barber Shop for crew cuts. Bing was a good guy, and although the haircut was a dollar, he'd give us a dime back to buy ice cream. Our feet seldom saw shoes during the summer. We always found our own entertainment; it wasn't our parents' job to entertain us.

Normally I'd help around the house in the morning. We had chickens and I'd gather the eggs or clean the chicken coop. On Saturdays, I'd deliver eggs to a few customers on my bicycle. Once the work was done, I was gone for the day, unless we got hungry. In that case, two or three of us would show up at one of our homes for a sandwich. We would often set up lemonade or Kool Aid stands. Sometimes we'd plan a yard circus or carnival, charging admission to other youngsters.

When I was about eleven or twelve, I got a paper route. I delivered the Rochester Times Union to about twenty-six customers throughout Arkport. I usually netted about $2.50 each week. I can still remember all of my customers and even the smell of each one's home. When we needed to supplement our incomes, my friends and I would look for pop bottles and redeem them at the grocery store for two, three, or five cents.

Chapter 3

TIMMERMAN

We lived next door to the Timmerman family. There was a huge cherry tree that sat on the property line and I loved climbing it. What I loved even more was hanging out at the Timmermans. They had a goldfish pond and a large garden similar to the one my Mom kept. Mr. Timmerman, known as Tim to most people, was a cool guy. He chewed tobacco and smoked cigars. He was a good baseball player, fisherman and hunter, and even kept chickens. He grew his own popcorn. It was normal for me to follow him around for hours. He'd often play catch with me. His son, Timmy, was at least ten years older than me, but he spent time with me as well. He taught me how to throw a baseball, field a ball, and hit the ball with a bat. He and I often played catch together. Sometimes after chores were done, Old Tim would invite me into the house. This was a treat because he would show me the Indian artifacts he'd found in the field behind his house. When I got older, young Tim would show me how to find arrowheads, axes, and other Indian artifacts. We'd walk for hours in the freshly plowed field.

An invitation into the house usually meant popcorn. Old Tim always wore a hat, but within his house, he'd remove his cap and expose a bald head. This was a sign to me that he was going to fix his homegrown popcorn. I loved the whole thing, the smell, the anticipation and the delicious taste. What fun, so honest and pure. I relish those memories to this day; they were some of the best memories of my childhood.

Even work was fun at the Timmermans. They rented a small piece of muck land on which they grew lettuce and onions. They would tie twine around the cuffs of their trousers to keep the black dirt out. I'd feel like a big shot whenever they would ask me to help them weed their plot.

During deer season, I'd love to look in Tim's garage to see the deer hanging and skinned. When I was old enough to hunt, I'd be invited to drive to Haskinsville to hunt with them. Even as I grew older, I'd spend time over there.

Sunday mornings were particularly exciting, as local men would spend hours pitching horseshoes. I'd hang around listening to all the stories and if they were "short" a man, I'd be asked to fill in. I actually got quite good at the game and Old Tim laughed whenever I'd top an opponent.

I was in high school when I learned that Mr. Timmerman had died. He was only sixty-four years old and he had a heart attack while bowling. He died as he had lived, having fun. I took his death hard because I lost a friend. Even today, I wish I could have lived more like Roswell "Tim" Timmerman. He lived simply, was happy with what he had, and above all, he seemed to enjoy life.

Chapter 4

BAD LUCK IN SPORTS

School had always been fun for me and was the center of my social activities.

As I grew older, sports, more particularly baseball, were my passion. Only a few people knew how good I was. I could field a ball, hit and play multi-positions. I also could think. I knew the plays and what to do with the ball. A bunch of us joined the Grasshopper League in Hornell and my performance was outstanding. When it came time to be recruited into little league, I wasn't chosen, even though I was an outstanding player. I was ten years old, the coaches wanted eight and nine-year olds. I was devastated. I continued playing sandlot ball and participating in Monday's "Boy's Night" and Saturday's "Boy's Mornings."

At age thirteen, I was playing soccer when an opponent and I both headed for the ball. I thought he would "chicken out," but as soon as we met everything suddenly went black. Seeing the ball was the last thing I remember before waking up on the field in sheer pain. Coach McCaffery carried me to Doc Wolfgruber's office. Doc said that my leg wasn't broken, just bruised. Even today Duffy, Ron and some of the other boys that

13

were playing that night can remember hearing my leg break. I was in excruciating pain all night.

The next day Coach Frank Rose stopped by my house. The Coach was a tough guy, a former World War II fighter pilot, respected by all of us. "Put on your sneakers," he said, "Okay now walk." I tried to please him but couldn't. After he departed, I told my Mom to take me to the hospital. An hour later, I had a plaster cast on up to my hip. People didn't sue in those days. Playing soccer with no protective gear such as shin guards would have made a perfect case of negligence. If I had broken my leg today, I would have received a sizable jury award. The only thing my Dad asked was that the school bus pick me up and take me home.

This incident not only injured me physically, but psychologically as well. I was unable to play baseball my freshman year since my leg was not fully healed. By the time I was a sophomore, I had not been involved in athletics for a year or more. When I reported for baseball practice as a sophomore, two things happened. Lyle McCaffery was no longer the coach, which left Harry Aldrich, our out of shape Guidance Counselor, with the job. I'm sure Harry applied for the job for the money rather than the love of the game. He knew nothing about the players' abilities. The first time I stepped up to bat, John Hubric threw me a curve ball. I practically dove out of the batter's box and it was a strike. I was scared and afraid of being hurt. That's what the broken leg did to me. I ended up quitting the team and my athletic career ended before it even started.

Chapter 5

FUELING LOVE AND FUELING GRIEF

It was about this time that I discovered girls. With teenage hormones kicking in, my buddies and I found "girl watching" to be our main attraction. We built a cabin in the woods located in the center of our village. This area is now a public park with tennis courts, pavilions, and picnic areas, but back then it was our private hideaway. We had a kerosene stove and a supply of *Playboy* magazines. At least a half dozen of us would hang out there smoking cigarettes and talking about our plans for the future or drooling over the latest centerfold.

During my teenage years, my Father started to put me to work on his potato farm. I wasn't much of a farmer and was not a reliable "tractor man," so I usually worked as a laborer doing menial jobs. The farm always had three or four full time black men who worked for us all year long. During the harvest, we would house fifty or more migrant workers.

I knew many of these black families from the time I was young. I found men like James Thomas, Ray Morris, Charlie Rose, Joe Parker, and Clara and Hosie Wortham interesting and was fortunate to have had this insight into the lives of another part of our society. When I was able to drive, I operated a "Cab

Service" transporting the black workers from the farm to Hornell to shop. I also became somewhat of a "Banker;" I would lend them $5 and get $7 in return. They would get paid on Saturday and be broke by Monday, so this was a lucrative endeavor for me, and a valuable service to them.

By the time I reached 9th grade, I had gone from being a good student to being a lousy one. My best friend, Wink Wolfgruber and I found life to be one big joke. We laughed over everything and appeared to give little thought to the future. We were "happy go lucky!" Our dream was to one day own a sports car dealership. Instead of discussing Math or French, we'd lust over some of the better-looking girls in the class. We were thrown out of French language lab after singing on the tape recorder and doing a mock radio interview. We made one mistake; we forgot to erase the tape.

Wink and Doc Wolfgruber, 1964

We each failed two or three classes as freshmen. I had to make up Algebra and History at summer school. Wink's folks sent him off to a private school in Wilkes Barre, Pennsylvania the next year.

In retrospect, I believe we were both well above normal intelligence and in some ways ahead of our time in our way of thinking. We did not accept everything taught to us, nor did we think conforming to academia's blueprint for success was necessarily the best way.

In the '50s and '60s young high school graduates had limited choices. Teachers and guidance counselors dictated what "box" a person would fit. Girls could become teachers, nurses or housewives and those with poorer grades would be secretaries. Boys, if they were really bright and motivated, would be pushed toward law, engineering, or medicine. The next level of achievers would become school teachers, and the lowest level of academic achievers would be told to go in the military, to trade school, or to work.

Those of us remaining were "different." We dismissed academic concepts and chose to figure out life for ourselves. Some refer to this as the school of hard knocks. Boys like myself, Chuck, Jay and others fell into that category. Surprisingly, looking back at my own graduating class, I find some of the most successful members in life come from that category. Jay Voorhees learned civil engineering by working in the field and eventually became part owner of a construction company. Charlie Schwarz learned that he had a knack for computers and became a computer expert in the Silicon Valley.

I was good at what I did and learned by trial and error. I loved the business field and I worked hard, studied my chosen career by taking numerous courses and passing difficult state and Federal exams. I eventually became not only a licensed insurance broker, but also a Registered Investment Advisor and an active real estate investor.

Boys like myself, Wink, Chuck and Jay may not have been motivated students, but we were gifted with the ability to articulate ourselves, to relate well to others, to make friends easily, and to gain their trust.

Nevertheless, at that moment in time I suspected that my parents were more than a little concerned about me. I was not only a disappointment as a student, but I also became somewhat rebellious. They didn't approve of some of my friends and wondered what would become of me.

My sister used this opportunity to fuel the fire. She lowered my self-esteem by telling me that I was stupid because I couldn't understand Algebra. If I got in trouble at school, my Mother knew by the time I got home. It gave Jean such pleasure to chip away at my self worth. My sister put me down for so many years that I was aware of even my slightest flaw.

I vividly remember one of my first "girlfriends" from Hornell. Her name was Mary Ann; she was a pretty Italian girl several inches taller than I was. It was a big deal having a girlfriend from out of town. Jean pointed out that my girlfriend was taller than I was and that she was a "greasy wop."

In my sophomore year, I changed from a college entrance curriculum to business education. I really felt that I would like to be a businessman. I was impressed with the salesmen in their suits, ties, and especially nice cars. It seemed like a better life than what I saw on the farm. My Father worked from early morning until dark and even some Sundays. He would come home dirty and tired. I know that he loved his job, the independence and being in the fresh air. I had a tremendous amount of respect for him. He was a successful and prosperous farmer.

My Father was a wonderful, kind, patient man who worked hard for his family and never complained. However, farming just wasn't in my blood. A sales job or owning a small business was my career goal. I enjoyed my business courses and did well. Earl Levengood, my business teacher, encouraged me and helped boost my self-esteem by telling me I had the personality and aptitude for a successful career in business.

I enjoyed school and loved the social aspects. It wasn't until after my sophomore year that the "Frog" began to transform into a "Prince." I began to grow and physically fill out. I began to feel a sense of respect from my peers. I made friends easily, began to gain attention from the girls and I knew everyone.

My sister finally graduated, so by my junior year, I could enjoy school without having to worry about her antics. As a senior, I spent half of my day at Arkport and the afternoons at Hornell High School as part of an experimental program. This allowed me to meet more people at the new school. I was in heaven! I was now considered a good-looking guy even though I never fully believed it because I'd been put down by my sister for so long. I got dates easily with some of the most attractive girls. Looking back, I wish I'd been more sensitive to their feelings instead of hurting some of them.

Eventually I met a girl named Polly who became my first true love. Polly was two years younger than me, but mature for her age. We had wonderful times together. This was the first time in my life that I actually felt I loved a girl.

In June of 1965, I graduated from high school. Polly came to my graduation. I had decided to go to college locally in order to get a car of my own. Dad actually bought a 1960 Valiant for me my senior year. It was nicknamed the green rat. Wink was home from private school for the summer and had just gotten a Honda motorcycle from his parents. We had a great time together. When Wink and I were together, we acted crazy. We were always joking and laughing at things that others might not find amusing.

This caused some friction in my relationship with Polly. At the same time, I believe her mom and dad found this was the time to encourage her to end our relationship, which was becoming "too serious." In July, she left for Nantucket with her family. Wink and I continued our carefree lifestyle. I worked on the farm days and partied every night. On July 12, we celebrated my eighteenth birthday by going to the Blue Goose in Wayland, N.Y. for my first "legal" drink. Wink was living at his family's cottage on Loon Lake; my folks had a summerhouse on one of our farms. As we departed at the end of the evening, I had no idea that this would be the last time I saw my best friend alive.

The following morning Wink was hit by a school bus while riding his Honda to summer school. This was before helmet laws. He was in the hospital for almost two weeks. No visitors were allowed. He finally died just shy of his eighteenth birthday. The days that followed were a painful blur to me. I attended the funeral, but remember little else. I felt like I had lost a part of me. I felt alone. I began to drink and did things that were not characteristic of me. My relationship with Polly ended.

Chapter 6

REAPING THE WHIRLWIND

Jean dropped out of Nursing School that summer, married a guy named Mike and became pregnant. Mike was a real nice fellow, seven years her senior who had just gotten home from the Army. As much as I liked Mike, I couldn't help but feel sorry for him; his life with Jean would not be easy.

I started at Alfred State College in the fall of 1965, but wasn't a motivated student. I partied too much and spent more time at the Beacon Inn than I did in the classroom. I was still suffering from my loss of Wink and my lost relationship with Polly. While in college, I became friends with a kid named Greg Zimmer. Greg was quiet and somewhat shy so I kind of "took him under my wing." He loved to party and raise hell. We both did that well, but failed miserably in academics. During my freshman year at Alfred State, I met Sandy Nikl, a pretty blonde haired nursing student with big brown eyes. The first time I saw her walking through the campus, I told Greg, "I'm going to marry that girl." I didn't even know her name! She was a Slovak girl from Endwell, N.Y Eventually a romance blossomed and I fell in love again.

By the end of the school year, both Greg and I were asked not to return. My relationship with Sandy also came to an end. These were the turbulent '60's; the war was raging in Vietnam, boys were burning their draft cards, and there was racial unrest in the South. There was also the constant threat of a Nuclear Holocaust. Us recent high school graduates were scared; there were so many decisions facing us. Many of us handled it all by living like there was no tomorrow.

My parents were disappointed in my performance at college, and the lack of direction in my life. I worked on the farm that summer and became physically strong. Bucky Roosa and I discussed joining the Navy, something I always wanted to do. Greg called and suggested I go in the Air Force with him. I seriously considered this until I got sick in Buffalo while taking the Air Force physical.

By the end of summer, I decided to get back into school and convinced my parents to pay for me to attend Rochester Business Institute. I had a good time living in the city and meeting new friends. I got a part time job while there, but continued partying as well. I learned a great deal about the business world while at RBI. Their instructors were actual attorneys, stockbrokers, insurance agents and so forth. It was a great opportunity to pick the brains of successful people in their chosen field rather than academics who simply taught theory out of textbooks. I did well, but Jean, of course, dismissed this by saying, "I know someone retarded who went there and got good grades."

During the spring of 1967, my friend Joe Sanderl and his girlfriend Patty Black introduced me to Patty's best friend, Lisa Savona. Patty and Lisa were from Long Island. She attended Bennett College, a private girls' college near Vassar College. As Joe and I drove down from Rochester, our first stop in town was the Millbrook Inn, a favorite hangout for the locals. We had a couple beers then drove over to the college. Lisa Savona was there as my date for the weekend. She was a gorgeous girl and we liked each other from the start.

The four of us spent the weekend together. Saturday evening we attended a private party sponsored by the college.

Little Eva of "Locomotion" fame was the performer for the evening. Joe and I both took turns dancing with her. During intermission, "Savie" and I went to my car, but within minutes security officers were directing us back inside. I hadn't realized Nuns ran Bennett College! "Savie" and I carried on a long distance romance; I learned that she modeled for *Mademoiselle* and *Glamour* magazines. Unfortunately the relationship ended about as quickly as it started. We were obviously from two different worlds.

In the autumn of 1967, I was back on the farm. I had become strong and it was a "macho" thing for me to try to outwork the black workers. Working on the farm during that fall harvest confirmed two things for me. Farm work was long and hard, and it was not a life I wanted. I remember unloading railroad cars full of seed potatoes with the help of one other man. We would stack five 100-pound bags on a handcart, push them to our flatbed truck, restack them, then take them to our warehouse and repeat the process. I could not envision myself doing this work forever. Although I was eligible for a farm deferment, I preferred two years of military service to a lifetime on the farm.

By now, several of my friends had been drafted. Chuck Schwarz was in Germany, and John Hubric was in Officer Candidate School. My cousin Tony was in Laos with the Special Forces. Ronnie Strobel was home on leave from the Army where he served as a clerk. He and I were drinking one afternoon and began talking about the Army. The more we talked, the more we drank. By the end of our conversation, I was gung ho about going into the Army. So, intoxicated, I drove to the draft board in Bath, N.Y. and told them I was volunteering for the draft, a decision that changed my life. I suppose that by volunteering I spared someone else's son or husband from Arkport or the surrounding areas from being drafted. This meant I would only have to do two years in the military. It also meant I would have no choice as to job training. I thought, "What are my chances of ever ending up as an Infantryman in Vietnam?" After all, Chuck was in Germany, Ron was a clerk, and John was an ordinance officer. Within a few days, I received my "Greetings from the President of the United States."

Until the day they died, I never told my folks the truth about having volunteered. Earlier that summer I met a group of nursing students from St. James Hospital. The girls were all nice Catholic girls. I started dating some of them, but had a special relationship with Mary Nolan. Mary was from Geneva, N.Y. She was one of eight children. I would have liked to have had a more serious relationship, but my ego got in the way. I had told Mary that I didn't want a girlfriend while I was in the Army because it wouldn't be fair to her. I had hoped she would still say she would wait for me, but she didn't.

Dave Roberts, a good looking athletic guy whom all the nursing students knew, had lost both legs to a VC booby trap that summer. I believe this was on Mary's mind and discouraged her from having a serious relationship with me. On October 20, 1967, my Father drove me to Bath where I waited with the other young men for our bus ride to Syracuse for induction.

Many years later my daughter asked how I felt about my actions. I'm sure when I sobered up I thought "what the hell have I done," but I also was glad that a decision was made. My life was no longer on hold. I knew what I'd be doing for the next two years. I truly believe that had I not gone in the service, I would have always wondered what the military was all about. Unfortunately, that same curiosity went beyond serving in the military. Somehow deep down inside, I knew I would end up in Vietnam as a combat soldier. It was my fate, my destiny. Deep down, I wanted to serve my country like my Father had during World War II.

Chapter 7

WHICH CUP IS THE PEANUT UNDER?

I was sent to Ft. Dix, N.J. for Basic Training. What a rude awakening! Instead of coming home at 3 or 4 a.m. after a night of partying, I was standing in formation saluting a flag I couldn't see. It was a nightmare! Since we were in a seven-week cycle in order to get us home for Christmas, all our training was accelerated. We were up at 4 a.m. and in bed at 7 p.m.

Ft. Dix got cold and the sand wasn't great for walking. My closest friend in boot camp was Jay Schmid. Jay was twenty-six years old and almost escaped the draft. His family owned the Trojan Condom Company. Jay worked days in the family business while earning a degree in the evening. He told me that he had just purchased a Corvette and recently inherited a house in Germany. All this was on hold for the next two years. Jay was the only male "heir apparent" to the Schmid family business. Somehow we helped one another through the forced marches, gas warfare training, physical training, drill and ceremonies. Two weeks before the end of Basic, we were given our orders for future individual training. I was told I was being sent to Ft. Jackson, S.C. for Advanced Infantry Training. Jay's orders were worse; he was also in the Infantry, but he was going to "Tigerland," Ft. Polk, Louisiana.

I was scared. The next day we had an orientation with a WAC. A lady Sergeant met with each of us individually and offered us new career schools. She offered to send me to Supply School and asked me to sign a form. This sounded great to me.

"You mean all I have to do is sign this form? I don't have to spend any more time in the Army?"

"Oh yes. You must commit to another year."

When I refused, she said, "OK, take your chances in the Infantry because they'll send you to Vietnam."

The next day I got a newspaper clipping from my Mom. My childhood friend Freddy Kemp had been killed at Quang Tri serving with the Marines. I thought long and hard about what the WAC said.

"Jay, I'm signing up for the third year in order to go to School instead of the Infantry."

"Don't do it," Jay shouted, "There is nothing worth spending another year in here. I'll take my chances in Vietnam before I spend another day in the Army."

He was convincing; I made the decision that I'd go into the infantry and hope that by some quirk my fate would change.

I knew what was happening to me, yet a part of me didn't believe it. Somehow I felt I'd get out of this. Yet another part of me still knew I'd end up in Vietnam. A part of me wanted the experience of combat and to be a part of history. That same part of me would always have been disappointed if I didn't fulfill my destiny.

My Father drove to New Jersey to pick me up after boot camp, which ended a week before Christmas of 1967. I appreciated that very much. I could sense that he looked at me much differently and could see a real change in me. My Mother cried when she saw me enter her kitchen in my dress greens. I saw Ron Strobel, the guy who convinced me to volunteer, and we spent New Year's Eve together at the American Legion. Ron told me that he had received his orders for Vietnam. I enjoyed my leave, but realized there was nothing in Arkport for me so I was ready to report to Ft. Jackson.

Never having been in the South, I didn't know what to expect. I thought it would be hot. I was surprised to quickly discover that South Carolina winters can be damn cold. I was assigned to Bravo Company 3rd Brigade; 48% of us were white and 52% were Black or Hispanic. I soon learned that many of the whites were tough street kids from the cities. It was a tough bunch and I learned not to look at anyone the "wrong" way to avoid any type of confrontation.

We were trained by "Shake'n Bake" Sergeants. These were soldiers who were selected to go to Combat Leaders School after AIT (Advanced Infantry Training). Upon completion of the school, they were promoted to Sgt. E-5 or Staff Sgt. E-6. There was one stipulation; they had to agree to a tour of combat duty in Vietnam. This program solved the Army's problem of a shortage of NCO's (Non Commissioned Officers) due to casualties. The training at Ft. Jackson lasted twelve weeks. Our training was hard; we had PT (Physical Training) three times a day. Between the farm work, boot camp, and now Infantry Training, I was in the best physical condition I'd ever experienced.

We trained with the Army's full arsenal of weapons: the M16, the M-60 machine gun, the .50 caliber machine gun, M-79 grenade launchers, the LAW an Anti-Tank weapon, the .45 caliber pistol, the Claymore mines, and many others. In addition, we learned about guerrilla warfare; not only our tactics, but also the tactics "Charlie" used against us. There was not as much harassment in AIT as there had been in boot camp. I felt like everyone was concerned that we learn what was necessary in order to stay alive in combat.

As trainee infantrymen we knew this was serious business and we were conscientious students willing to learn whatever we could to stay alive in Vietnam. We knew that when this training was completed most of us would be sent to war. At the completion of our twelve weeks, we had one final exercise; it was called RVN (Republic of Vietnam) Training and it lasted three days. We were on trucks when "VC" (Vietcong) attacked our convoy. This mock battle included firefights, capturing prisoners, evading the enemy, and all other simulations of combat.

At the completion of our training in March of 1968, we assembled outside to receive our orders. In most cases, it was not a matter of if we'd go to Nam, but of what unit we would join. There would be some exceptions in the case of men who had brothers already in Vietnam. Normally they would be sent to Korea or Germany. A few of our group would be chosen for the Combat Leaders School at Ft. Benning.

As they started calling names and assigning units, they got to the point of calling for Combat Leaders. I had a good rapport with the Cadre and had done well in my training, but I was still surprised to find that I was one of the few chosen for the Combat Leaders School. I was more surprised to learn that I was one of four men out of over one hundred, who were selected to become Drill Corporals. This supposedly meant we'd never see Vietnam and never work in our eleven Bravo MOS (Military Occupational Specialty). I was ecstatic. Steve Stoddart, one of my buddies, was also selected for Drill Corporal School.

That evening as I crawled into my bunk, I discovered it was filled with shaving cream. Apparently some of my "buddies" weren't as ecstatic about my orders as I was. I know they were waiting for me to do something; instead I said, "F--k it. I'll never see you bastards again after tomorrow," and I fell asleep. Steve and I flew to Ft. Lauderdale that night to visit his girlfriend. I'd never been to Florida and enjoyed the time away from the Army. I went from Florida to Arkport to visit my family and to tell them my good news. When I returned to Ft. Jackson, I was told Drill Corporal School was closed and that I would be training Cadre at the 2nd Brigade, which trained clerk typists. We would have Buck Sgt. stripes sewn on our uniforms and although we were PFC's, we'd be promoted as soon as we had sufficient time in service. I reported to the C.O. (Commanding Officer), Captain John Shook. I saluted him and as we talked, I told him I would do my best. It was at this point that he advised me that my orders had been changed. Shock came over me as he said that I was to join the 5th Mechanized Infantry Brigade at Ft. Carson, Colorado. We would train together for ninety days and then the entire Unit would go to Vietnam.

Chapter 8

DRILL SERGEANT BLUES

Captain Shook must have seen my disappointment or perhaps I made a good first impression.

"I'm tired of losing personnel. They send me people then take them away. Senka, you want to go to Officer Candidate School, don't you?"

"Not really sir. That would mean another year in the Army."

"That's OK Senka. You go to O.C.S. That way they'll put a hold on you and cancel these orders. When the time comes that you are called for O.C.S., just tell them you've changed your mind."

"Yes sir," I replied, snapped a salute and headed for Post Headquarters.

I later met the other Sergeants I'd be working with; all were Nam Vets. Sgt. E-6 Bruce Pealer was a tough straight talker from Tennessee. He was twenty-six years old, but looked much older. War has a way of aging a man. Sgt. Rigukis was a funny little guy who I thought had been wounded in action. I later learned he came home on emergency leave, to settle a divorce. While he was home, he "accidentally" shot himself on a rifle range and would not have to return to combat. The man I was closest to was Sgt. Willie Tucker, a black man from Anderson, S.C. Tucker had been wounded while serving with the 25th Infantry Division's "Wolfhounds" in Vietnam. He lost his right calf muscle.

Being a Drill Sgt. was hard work and we put in long hours, but it was better than being a "grunt" in Nam. I worked my butt off trying to be the best. Our day started early, at about 6 a.m. We got up, "broke starch" and put on our shiny boots and sparkling belt buckles. We got the troops up and had a company formation in front of our barracks. We then gave the troops time to clean the barracks before we marched them to PT (Physical Training). I would normally stand on the podium in the parking lot leading the troops in the Army's daily dozen.

John, Drill Sgt. in Ft. Jackson prior to Nam

Occasionally Lt. King, the Training Officer, would conduct PT. King was a pimply-faced red head from the streets of Brooklyn. His military bearing was terrible especially for an officer. His uniforms were usually wrinkled and his boots were never shined properly. He had a deep voice for a little guy. He also had a reputation for being tough, supposedly a street fighter. Many of the trainees from New York City knew him from the streets. Lt. King and I seemed to have a mutual respect for one another. I sense the same was true of Captain Shook and me.

Willie Tucker and myself did the majority of the work done in our Company.

Sgt. Pealer was married and went home to his wife each night, and Sgt. Regukis was a joke; eventually they made him a truck driver someplace. Sgt. Willie Tucker and I became close friends. Race made no difference because I was raised with other African Americans on the farm. Somewhere along the line, friction had developed between some of the southern soldiers who were Company Clerks and myself. It began over an Article Fifteen, which was a form of non-judicial punishment under the Code of Military Justice. It was one of the few punishments we Drill Sergeants had available for infractions such as insubordination by a trainee. Only once did I take part in a Court Martial. In my opinion that trainee was a spoiled, overweight Jewish boy from New York City who paid another trainee to lie at the trial. Afterward Captain Shook suggested I take Pvt. Silverfarb down to the athletic field and beat the crap out of him. I gave it serious consideration, but in the end discarded that idea.

The Company clerks, Bob Lankford in particular, disliked typing Article Fifteens and told me to stop issuing them. I wasn't about to take orders from Lankford so I told him to "F--k off." There were enough other people I had to take orders from; why take them from a lowly PFC? This action began an alienation between the southern clerks, who eventually got me shipped to Vietnam, and myself. I don't think these southerners appreciated my friendship with Sgt. Tucker, a Yankee from New York and a black man, either.

I had one strong ally and that was Captain Shook. He protected me; I believed we had a mutual respect for one another; that and the fact that I ran a "tight ship" and did the bulk of the work. I made friends at Ft. Jackson; many of the instructors at the Clerk Typist School were great guys, but those were the instructors from the northern states such as New York and Massachusetts. Frank Foster from Farmville, Virginia, ironically, was my closest friend. He and I had many good times together.

I continued to work long hours with little social life. I'd occasionally go to Jimmy's, a bar within walking distance of the main gate. There I would drink 3.2 % (low alcohol content) beer until I was sufficiently intoxicated. Jimmy's had an intimidating bouncer who weighed about 400 pounds with a full beard and shaved head. At the conclusion of my visits, I'd speculate about "kicking his ass," but in the end I'd think about it and make the wise choice of leaving quietly. "Beer Muscles" can get a soldier in trouble.

The situation worsened over time; I was getting sick of the "bullshit" at Ft. Jackson. The long hours, inspections, and parades, but I knew it was better than the alternative of serving as a grunt in South Vietnam. By now there was more friction between some of the Southern Cadre and myself. Perhaps it was a cultural difference to some. Once Lankford, the clerk, told me I looked like a "hood" because I rolled the cuffs of my civilian shirt; apparently that wasn't cool in the South. Lt. Gil Few, the effeminate executive officer, seemed to side with the instructors. He never really harassed me, but he was cold towards me. He "had it made" since his home and family were just a few miles from Ft. Jackson. This was like a 9 to 5 job for him.

One real asshole in the Brigade was an instructor named Aaron Kinnard. He drove a new Mustang convertible and kissed anyone's ass to make rank. He had a reputation for having a big mouth. One evening he stopped in my room where a group of us were talking and made a rude remark to me. I lost my temper and roughed him up. It scared and embarrassed him. I later apologized, but I knew there would be repercussions against me. I just didn't know how damaging they would be or how they would change my life.

I had been at Ft. Jackson for eight or nine months now, six of them as permanent party. I was in excellent physical condition. I had done PT every day for almost a full year now. I would often challenge those trainees struggling with push-ups by doing mine with one hand. Every Saturday we put on dress greens and paraded around the Brigade field while Col. Van Oxx reviewed us on his white horse. This spit polish, petty bullshit was really getting to me.

Frank Foster and I used to start drinking after the parade, but Frank had gotten shipped to Vietnam where he was serving as a clerk. Steve Stoddart and I started to hang out together; he tried to get me to volunteer for Vietnam with him. I always assumed it was just "beer muscles," but then one day he told me that he had done it. He had given up his safe position at a training brigade to serve as a grunt in Nam. So now I was alone weekends and would sometimes sleep from Saturday noon until Monday. I would sporadically wake up to eat. In retrospect, I may have been depressed, or possibly just lonely.

Shortly after, my name came down on a levy for Vietnam. I knew someone was behind it and Captain Shook concurred that I apparently made some enemies with the clerks. In the Army even a lowly Pvt. Clerk had access to files and orders and could raise hell with personnel such as 1st Sergeants and officers. I immediately filed for "Sole Surviving Son" status. I honestly felt I qualified since my biological Father had died as the result of "war incurred maladies." This excuse saved my ass for the time being. It would take weeks to learn if I was given this status so my name came off the levy.

Chapter 9

ROMANCE AND NAM

I was so sick of the place that I almost signed on for Special Forces Training. They were looking for soldiers with 11B MOS to apply to Special Forces. My cousin Tony was serving with them so I knew a little about it. I knew I would have to attend airborne training before entering the training at Ft. Bragg. I was in magnificent physical shape and thought that by the time I finished training the war might be over. In the end, I thought about what my friend Jay Schmid had said and decided I didn't want to add another year to my tour of duty.

One Saturday night I walked to Jimmy's Bar. Willie Tucker said that he might be there. I walked in, ordered a beer, and sat at a table alone. Many of my trainees were there having a good time. They were all friendly to me and I smiled and waved, but I could not fraternize with them. I noticed a table nearby that was occupied by civilians. There was one particularly attractive girl seated at the table. I watched as several of the trainees wandered to her table in the hopes of dancing with her. One after another they would return rejected. I ordered a few more beers as I sat alone watching the young people out having a good time. I waved to Willie Tucker who was dressed impeccably and displaying his talent as a dancer.

I couldn't take my eyes off the good-looking lady at the table. The trainees had long given up on a chance to dance with her and were replaced by some college boys who pursued her. One after another, she shot them down. When I ordered my next beer I felt someone watching me and turned to see this same woman watching me. Our eyes locked and instantly I knew we had connected in some way. Maybe she was curious why I sat alone. I really felt like dancing and had drank enough to build up my nerve. I thought I might embarrass myself in front of my trainees if she shot me down, but what the hell? So I walked over to her, ignoring the glances from the men at her table. Everyone in the place was watching me as I asked her to dance. The trainees yelled out, "Yeah, Sgt. Senka," as she walked to the dance floor with me.

Tucker was dancing near me with a big smile on his face. He said, "Damn J.T., you can dance. You're a Blue Eyed Soul." When the dance ended, the pretty Southern Belle minced no words.

"My name is Shirley Radford, I'm twenty-five years old, divorced, and I have a little boy."

"My name is John Senka, I'm twenty three (I was only twenty) and I have no problem with you having a son."

Shirley then invited me to join her table and introduced me to her friends. At the end of the evening, she gave me her phone number and invited me to call her.

After all these months, there was finally some sunshine in my life. I went to Columbia that weekend and met Shirley's family. Her dad was a fine Southern gentleman and her mom was hospitable. Her son was a little gentleman who shook hands with me. As for Shirley, she was more beautiful than I had remembered. The date was awkward since we double dated with the Supply Sergeant and his wife, with whom we had little in common. Without a car, I had no choice. I enjoyed my date with Shirley and felt I could really get serious even though she was unknowingly five years older than I was.

The following Monday, we learned Captain Shook was leaving. He was going to train as a Chopper Pilot. I knew then that my days were numbered.

Captain Shook said, "Why don't you be my Crew Chief, Senka?" He then laughed and said, "I'll finish my second tour in Nam before you ever got there." I wasn't so sure. We had a party for Shook that ended in a fistfight between Lt. King and Sgt. Pealer. Bruce Pealer was told to go on leave. Our new Commanding Officer was a Major Aubrey McGrady who had just returned from Vietnam. McGrady was a Southern boy and I could tell immediately that the clerks had already gotten to him. His attitude towards Sgt. Tucker and me was not good. He insinuated that we weren't doing our jobs. It was pretty small of him to act this way and be manipulated by Spec. 4 and Spec. 5 clerks. There was no question that he would never fill Captain Shook's shoes.

I knew I no longer wanted to stay, so I wasn't upset when I learned that my application for "Sole Surviving Son" status had been rejected a few days later. I'd take Vietnam over working with these people. My only regret was that my relationship with Shirley had to come to an abrupt end. The word was out that I was going to Vietnam. The latest training cycle was ending and many of these trainee clerks had received orders for Vietnam. Most of them were scared and upset. I tried to cheer most of them by calling them "Remington (typewriter) Rangers" and told them they'd be working in air-conditioned offices. I said, "How'd you like to be in my shoes?" They all knew I was infantry trained and would see combat. I was still a Private First Class in actual rank and I was upset that I hadn't made Specialist 4 yet.

My name was submitted as soon as I was eligible, but there were always more names than there were openings. Just before I departed, Lt. King stopped me.

"Sorry Sgt. Senka, you didn't get the promotion."

"I don't give a damn. I've been filling an E-6 slot since I got here and as far as I'm concerned I'm the best NCO in the entire battalion and you and everyone else knows it."

King looked at me and said "Sir." Realizing my obvious disrespect, I replied, "Sir." He then shook my hand and handed me my promotion. I knew going to Vietnam as an E-4 would be advantageous and it would take little time to make Sergeant E-5.

Chapter 10

ENGAGEMENT TO LOVE AND WAR

Around the first of September 1968, my orders were cut; I cleared post and decided I wouldn't spend even one extra day here. I started my thirty-day leave. Instead of going home, I flew to Ft. Campbell, Kentucky to visit close friends from my village, John and Bev Hubric. John was an officer at Ft. Campbell.

John and John Hubric during the thirty-day leave
at Ft. Campbell

On previous visits, I had met a German girl named Annalisa Belka. She was pretty and apparently liked me. I thought the world of the Hubrics and wanted to see them before leaving for Vietnam. I got drunk in Atlanta, missed my flight after an eight-hour wait and ended up taking a bus from Memphis to Clarksville. The only thing that arrived at Nashville was my duffel bag. I called John from a pay phone at Ft. Campbell. I was broke and my khakis were a mess from having slept in them on the bus. I needed sleep desperately. No dice, John insisted we hang out and talk over a bottle of Jack Daniels "Green Label." We got loaded and took Bev and Annalisa to the Officers Club that night. The whole week was a party. I called Ft. Jackson and told them to send my paycheck to John's house.

John on leave

I needed money to get home. I had inadvertently forgotten to tell my folks about my detour and later learned my Dad had called the Post Provost Marshall and was told I had cleared Post and was on orders for Vietnam. They had all kinds of thoughts. Perhaps I'd run off to Canada or had been in an accident. Our local Sheriff told my Dad to wait seven days after which he would put out a twenty-one State all points bulletin.

A few days later, my Mom saw Bev's mom in the grocery store and she told her that I was in Tennessee. I now had three weeks of leave remaining and decided to return to Arkport. I began to contemplate the seriousness and reality of my situation. The reality of the situation was that I was indeed going to Vietnam, and my job would be that of a combat infantryman. I realized that this would be a hard, miserable existence for a whole year and that I could be maimed or killed.

When John asked me if I ever heard from Sandy Nikl, the girl I dated at Alfred State, I said, "Yes. We write once in awhile, but I'll try to see her when I go home." I called my sister and asked her to call Sandy for me to see if she'd like to see me when I got home.

It felt good being home. My Mother and Father had built a beautiful new home while I was gone. Nothing had changed much in town. Many of my friends were in the military. Those still home had either married or were still dodging the draft. I had changed though. I no longer shared the same interests as my friends. I drove to Endwell the first Friday I was home to see Sandy and to bring her back with me. I wore a three-piece business suit, which was a welcome change from green fatigues and black boots. I sported a military style haircut much different from the hairstyles of my civilian peers. Sandy's dad complimented me on it. When Sandy came down the stairs, she was as pretty as I had remembered and when we entered my Father's car she slid next to me. It was as if time had stood still and our feelings for one another had not changed.

We returned to Arkport and stayed up into the early morning hours talking. Prior to turning in for the night, I asked her to marry me and she said yes. I was ecstatic. To many, this might have seemed sudden or unusual. In times of war, people make quick decisions because there is no time to do otherwise. Under normal circumstances, we may have taken things slower, enjoying our time together. There was no time though and I knew I loved Sandy and I did not want to lose her. I wanted to know there was someone waiting for me to come home.

John and fiancée, before leaving for Nam

The next morning, I told my Mom the news and she was thrilled because she liked Sandy, and was disappointed that we had previously gone our separate ways. She told me to drive to the farm to tell my Dad. Dad was very pleased and asked; "Do you have money for an engagement ring?" I told him how much I had and he suggested I spend a little more to get a better ring. "After all, you only do this once" he said. He offered to lend me some money and I agreed to repay him. We drove to Hornell and I asked Sandy to choose the ring she wanted. She glowed when I placed the ring on her finger and her beautiful brown eyes sparkled whenever she looked at it. She called her folks to tell them the news and before my leave was over, Mom had her family over for dinner.

All too soon my leave was over and the time for me to go to Vietnam had arrived. I had just turned twenty-one and spent the final afternoon of my leave at the local American Legion saying goodbye to my friends and whoever else was around. Bill Haines, a shell of a man and a known draft dodger, said, "How can you be so calm? Aren't you scared?" The room turned silent. I looked Bill in the eyes and said, "I'm scared shitless" and with that departed.

I went back to the house for dinner with my family. I put on my dress greens and posed for pictures with my Mom, Dad, and younger brothers Joey and Bobby. I packed my duffel bag in preparation for my departure the next morning. I knew I'd get little sleep tonight. So many thoughts went through my head. Would I ever see this house again or my family? Would Sandy ever see me? Would I ever return to the Village I loved? I ran my hand over the paneled walls of the hall in an almost sacred gesture.

Dad and Mom, night before leaving for Nam

As I lay in bed, my Mother entered the room. I pretended to be asleep. She touched my hair and petted my head. This had to be a heart wrenching moment for her. I'm sure she was thinking that she would be losing her son as she had her Father and first husband. The next morning, I awoke and thus began an acting job worthy of an Academy Award. I was cheerful, pleasant and exceptionally upbeat. I heard on the news that President Johnson had stopped the bombing. A letter arrived from my old friend Jay Schmid who was already in Vietnam. The letter was to the point, "This place is bad news." When my Mom inquired about the letter, I told her, "Jay said things in Vietnam aren't as bad as the news media reports." I said goodbye to my brothers and Mom, Dad, Sandy, and I packed into Dad's Oldsmobile for the hour drive to Rochester.

I continued my performance; my Dad even commented that it seemed like I couldn't wait to get to Vietnam. All I could do was laugh. I hugged and kissed Mom who was crying and shook Dad's hand. I kissed Sandy and told them all that I would see them in a year. I was careful to have worn my sunglasses because as I waived goodbye with a smile on my face, tears were streaming down my cheek. I was scared as hell!

I didn't want to leave Sandy. I had been happier during the past three weeks than I had been in a long, long time. As the plane departed for Ft. Dix, I knew that I had to "suck it up," put my life behind me, and concentrate on soldiering so that I could return to the life I left behind. Years later my daughter commented about my "sucking it up." She said, "Dad, that's always been your attitude. You taught us that when things get bad, you have to learn to 'suck it up.'"

Chapter 11

THE ANGUISH OF DUTY

In the fall of 1968, I got to Ft. Dix and was assigned to a reception station. Ironically, it had been the autumn of 1967, one year ago, that I had first arrived at Ft. Dix, a green, wet-behind-the-ears recruit. I met another soldier, Bob Stein, who was also heading for Vietnam in the infantry. Bob had graduated from Ithaca College. He was a physical education teacher and he was petrified. We spoke with another GI who had come home from Vietnam on emergency leave. This guy told us that he had been in Nam six months, and it was horrible! He told us that there was no way he was going back there, even though those were his orders.

The next morning, I was prepared to start my journey for Southeast Asia when we were informed that our flight wasn't leaving until Monday. This meant I'd be stuck at Ft. Dix for the weekend with less than $5 in my pocket. Had I known this, I could have spent two or three more precious days with my loved ones. Mentally, the others and I were ready to leave and the long, boring, lonely hours ahead had a serious impact on us. It gave us time to think about where we were going. I was afraid of what was ahead of me. I was sad that I might never again see Sandy and my family. I walked over to my old basic training company thinking how a year before I'd been here. There were no familiar faces.

When I got back to the building where I was housed, I saw Bob pacing the floor.

"Bob, what's wrong?"

"John, I'm not going,"

"Not going?"

"I'm not going to Vietnam. I'm afraid. I've decided that I'm leaving for Canada."

I just stared at this young soldier who had bonded with me these past forty-eight hours. Bob was serious.

"John, why don't you come with me? We'll go together."

"I can't Bob. I'm scared also, but maybe we'll luck out in Nam."

That evening I had only a few coins left in my pocket. I felt a loneliness I'd never felt before. I spent the last of my money on a phone call to Sandy. When she answered I tried to speak, but no sound came out. I knew if I spoke, I'd start crying. The charade was over; in a shaky voice, I told her I loved her as tears streamed down my face. I could hear her crying on the other end. I had never before shared my feelings with anyone. From now on any further conversations with her would be by mail.

The next morning Bob still insisted he was not going, but when the time came he followed me on the airplane and sat next to me. There was no turning back now. We flew from Maguire Airbase in New Jersey to Tacoma, Washington where we refueled. We then took the northern route via Alaska and landed in Anchorage to again refuel. We were allowed to deplane in Alaska and I wandered around the airport, purchased some post cards, and mailed them to my family and Sandy. This was a long journey; none of us were in a rush to reach our destination. The plane was so quiet you could hear a pin drop. None of the GIs aboard felt like talking; we were too busy thinking about our past and contemplating what was waiting for us. Our next stop was Tachakowa Air Force Base in Japan where we were able to wander around until the airliner was loaded with fuel for the final leg of our journey.

On October 1, 1968, as our airplane entered Vietnam airspace, we were told that we would soon be landing at Tan Son Nhut and that we should run away from the aircraft in case the airport was being shelled. When the airplane came to a stop, we deplaned and ran into the blazing hot, humid, stinking air. This would be home for the next year unless we were killed or wounded sooner.

Chapter 12

LIFE IN THE FIELD

Bob Stein stuck pretty close to me as we went from one place to another. We spent our first night at the 90th replacement at Long Binh. The wooden building had steel bunks, but no mattresses. I asked someone about this and was asked, "What's your MOS?" "11 Bravo," I said. The guy laughed and said, "This is the best bed you'll have all year." I sacked out on the metal bedsprings for the night looking at unusual insects crawling on the walls. At about midnight, I was awakened by shelling and followed the others as they ran into a metal culvert outside.

The next day I was put on Kitchen Patrol. I thought those days were behind me. There were two Filipino girls, twins actually, that worked with me. They would look at me and giggle; finally, one day, they walked toward me and ran their fingers through my hair. It seems like blond hair was a curiosity to them. The third day while in formation, we were asked if any of us had a college education in business. I quickly raised my hand and the officer in charge said, "Good. We can use you in our finance office." I couldn't believe this! Bob, having heard this, grabbed the Captain and told him that he had a college degree. We were both told to report to the finance office in the morning and that we could use their mess hall that evening. Bob and I were in seventh heaven; our asses were saved!

Rather than changing our orders that night, the Captain waited until the next day. When we reported to the finance office, they told us we couldn't get assigned there and they had not received the Captain's order change. They said we had a critical Military Occupational Specialty and were needed in the field. Bob and I just stared at one another in disbelief. I got assigned to the 25th Infantry Division and Bob, if I remember correctly, went to the 5th Mechanized Infantry. I never saw him again. I flew to Cu Chi, Headquarters of the 25th Infantry Division.

I spent a few days at Cu Chi. We attended three days of infantry training, which was like a mini review session. We were issued our rifles and steel pots, along with jungle fatigues and boots. We had several orientations to get our inoculations in order, our personnel records straight, and even a meeting with the chaplaincy. I recall a priest giving us Catholics a gold religious medal to wear around our necks.   They were made of plastic so they wouldn't cause any noise on ambushes. One trooper stood up and said, "Father, I was always taught **thou shalt not kill**, and *now* you are telling us it is okay." The priest's answer shocked me as he told us, "This killing is necessary and not only is it okay, but no matter what happens, if you're killed, you can be certain that you will go to heaven." This was a complete contradiction to what I had been taught by priests my entire life.

In addition to our training and orientations, we did get some free time. I visited the PX and the steam bath, where the girls were pleased to see some more "cherry boys," the name given to soldiers new to the country. The following morning, I was put on a convoy heading to Charlie Co. 4th Battalion 9th Infantry. I didn't know my unit was nicknamed "Suicide Charlie" because of all the casualties they had incurred over the years.

A cocky little "Shake and Bake" Sgt. was on the truck with me. He was a short black kid who gave me the impression that he was above talking with an E-4. We hadn't driven for more than a half-hour when our convoy began receiving small arms fire. Instinctively we jumped out and took cover behind the deuce and ½'s wheel. It was over as quickly as it started, but it marked the beginning of my tour with the Manchus.

When we reached the fire support base, the C.O. was happy to see E-4 and E-5 replacements. This base had no buildings, only tents and bunkers. My newfound comrades walked around in boots, green skivies, and T-shirts. When they learned I was from New York; they took me to a fellow named Dave Briggs. Briggs was from North Collins, New York and the more we talked, the more we had in common. David had been a roommate at Williamsport College with two of my close friends from Arkport, Bill Ells and Jerry Clark. He had visited Arkport and Hornell and we had even dated the same girl. I liked Spec. 4 Briggs and we quickly became friends.

Afterwards, I was assigned to my squad and got acclimated as best I could. Our lives began to have a semblance of routine. We would patrol each day. It was not unusual to walk ten to fifteen miles in the blistering sun, temperature often reaching 112 degrees. When dark came, we would either go out on a platoon or squad size ambush or on a three man listening post. Although the procedures were routine, the substance of our duties was anything but routine. We lived in constant fear, whether that fear was conscious or not.

Whenever we departed our compound, exiting the "wire," we would "lock and load" our M16; it was then that the real fear and anxiety set in. We were now in "no man's land." "Charlie," our name for the enemy, could be anyplace: a sniper in a tree, hidden in a spider hole, or lying in ambush. If they weren't there in person, one of their booby traps would be, a punji pit (a covered pit containing sharp bamboo stakes), or something more sophisticated such as explosive devices hidden or buried, which would blow when stepped on or when a wire was tripped.

I usually prayed as I started out on any type of mission. When I was really scared, I recited the 23rd Psalm. I carried a prayer book that the priest at Cu Chi gave me; sometimes I recited a "prayer for the enemy" asking that I would not have to kill another human being. I even prayed that if I must die in battle that it would be quick and painless.

A grunt's day is long; we were awake most of the twenty-four hours. Occasionally one could catch a few hours sleep during the day, but at night it was usually an hour at a time, or four hours at the most. The heat was unbearable at times and we were thirsty and hungry. Most of us carried a couple canteens of water with flavored "fizzies" in them but the drinks would quickly become hot. The only cold drinks would be the soda and beer that came in on the daily re-supply convoy. We'd spin the cans in a block of ice, and the beverage would become ice cold. We could also dip our "steel pots" (helmets) into a well or stream, but the water might have been contaminated.

We ate breakfast in camp and usually got a hot meal at supper, but we ate C rations for lunch, which was usually while out on patrol. We became pretty creative in our cooking techniques and the C's tasted pretty good. Sandy sent me boned chicken in a can and Vienna sausages. I carried these in my pockets and ate them right out of the can. Every day was different and presented new challenges.

Chapter 13

DIRT, DEATH, AND DUTY

By mid November I had already experienced combat several times. One time we were pinned down in a cemetery and hop scotched from tombstone to tombstone as bullets cracked over our heads. I had also seen my share of GIs maimed by mines, booby traps, and other explosive devices. It got so bad that I'd wonder if I'd detonate something every step I took. One would be particularly anxious when having to run in a heavily booby-trapped area, like the day a helicopter was shot down with a Colonel on it and we had to secure it.

Even though I'd only been in Vietnam a couple of months, days seemed like weeks and weeks felt like years. It was easy to forget what day of the week it was. I recall being on an ambush in the pouring rain with mosquitoes the size of butterflies biting me. I'd think, "Man, this is Friday night. I should be at the Arkport Inn, or Burkhart's partying with my friends." Did I ever do that? Did I wear sweaters and blue jeans and comfortable shoes? Didn't I use great smelling after-shave? The difficult part was the realization that many of my friends were still doing this; they were out enjoying themselves.

Sandy would write to me often, as would my Mom and Dad. My sister even sent letters. Every GI waits for mail; it was the highlight of our day, and kept us connected to the world. I got accustomed to my new life and made friends with Hank Maul, a Mormon from Wyoming, Phil Glenn a lanky nineteen-year old from Arkansas, Jose Olea from Buffalo and others. We looked after one another in a way I never saw before or have seen since. The compassion eighteen, nineteen, and twenty-year old boys showed for one another was beautiful.

I remember, while on a patrol, I realized I had lost one of my canteens and was out of water. It was hot and I was thirsty, but I said nothing to anyone. I recalled my infantry training when we were taught to have "our shit together" and not to infringe on the next guy to bail you out. To this day, I still adhere to this philosophy. Just then a black guy named White said, "Senka, where's your water?" I told him that I'd lost my canteen in the jungle. Without a moment's hesitation, he handed me his canteen. I have never forgotten his kindness toward me and I always appreciate a cold drink on a hot day and think of that moment.

One of the things I tried to do was maintain a routine and a sense of civility. I shaved and brushed my teeth every morning. Every night I showered and washed my hair. Sometimes I'd use a stream, or drop my steel pot in a well, and at some bases we'd even have a sprinkler out in an open field. We'd line up stark naked while Vietnamese civilians would pass by. Any sense of modesty had been long lost. It was in one of these showers that I noticed the guy in front of me looked familiar. I began laughing as I recognized Danny Hartwell, one of my childhood friends from Arkport. Dan was a generator mechanic with a unit supporting the 25th. It was fantastic seeing a familiar face and chatting about the old days growing up in Arkport. I told Dan I'd see him the next day, as my platoon would be going out on night ambush.

Intelligence indicated that "gooks" were snooping around our fire support base recently during early morning hours. I doused myself with mosquito repellent and grabbed my usual arsenal of 25 M16 magazines (500 rounds), two hand grenades, and a claymore mine along with my poncho liner. We would shiver at 80 degrees at night, a drop of 30 degrees or more from our daytime temperatures. After establishing our ambush site we quietly waited for the little brown man or woman to infiltrate. After about three hours, we sprang the ambush; all hell broke loose. We killed no one and I personally saw no one out there. It made no difference to me; I was glad we all made it back to camp safely.

As we entered camp on November 23, 1968, I joked with Dave Briggs. Dave had just been appointed by Captain Winters, our Company Commander's RTO (radio operator). I said, "Dave, you have it made now." The entire Company was going out on patrol except for my platoon since we'd spent the night in the bush. I got cleaned up, ate, and cleaned my rifle when I finally got back to visit Danny.

He said, "John, what are you doing here? I heard your Company was pinned down."

"What the hell are you talking about?"

He explained that Captain Winters had led Charlie Company into an NVA Battalion size base camp. Captain Winters and Dave Briggs had both been killed, as well as most of the other members of Charlie Company. I couldn't believe what I was hearing. I returned to my bunker, and those of us in our platoon were told to "saddle up." We were being dropped into the battle.

Fear once again encompassed us, but we knew we'd want help if it were we pinned down out there. We reported to the departure area and were told to forget it. It was too risky to drop us in there. We did leave our ammo and other supplies which they did drop. I returned to be with Danny, and we listened to the battle on a field radio. A Corporal was now commanding the radio of Charlie Company. Many hours later, the massacre ended and the remainder of Charlie Company returned to our Fire Support Base, many in body bags. We were invited to view the bodies of our comrades, but I declined. David Briggs' death hurt me deeply, and the reality of the situation hit me between the eyes. If Dave could be killed, then anyone could be next, even me.

Sandy continued to write me, but I was finding it more and more difficult to relate to her letters. She would talk about our future, but I was no longer sure that there would be a future. I could not be certain I'd be here tomorrow. When she wrote that she knew how hard it must be for me, I got upset because she had no idea how bad the life of a grunt was, no one did. Only another grunt could relate to the heat, humidity, insects, thirst, hunger, lack of sleep, and fear. I no longer felt human; I had become an animal. When I was on patrol, my sense of smell became acute, my ears would almost perk up like that of a dog, my eyes would scan like those of a hawk or eagle. I no longer felt completely human. I was now comfortable in my environment. Living like this had become a way of life for us. The life I knew prior to Vietnam was only a memory, a vision of a distant past.

Thanksgiving was not much different than any other day, with the exception of a delicious turkey dinner we ate in the field. Half way through dinner, gas that was being dropped by an Air Force fighter plane was blown back on us. Few of us had gas masks so we covered our noses and mouths with whatever was available. There was a hell of a battle taking place and either Alpha Company or we would be attacked. We lucked out again. Charlie Company would act as a blocking force while Alpha Company engaged a battalion size unit of North Vietnamese Regulars (NVA).

As darkness approached, I was told to get a field radio and go out on Listening Post (LP). The more seasoned soldiers urged me not to go. "What am I supposed to do? I can't disobey an order, can I?" They said, "Call in your reports from here inside the compound." I knew I couldn't do that because that's not who I was. I followed the rules, I grew up in an era where we had respect for authority, I was responsible and a good soldier. In retrospect, perhaps I was "green" and naïve putting my honor before my safety.

As I prepared to exit the wire, I was warned, "Be careful, there are gooks out there." I didn't go too far out, but found a place in the brush to lay low for the night. We could hear the shelling and small arms fire in the distance. Suddenly I received a call on my radio, "Hey Spec do you smell dead gooks?" It was

"Hippie" Miller, a decorated Sergeant. Normally, someone like him would be put in the rear, but Miller pissed the brass off and he was now paying the price. "Miller, I can't answer that, I've never smelled dead gooks," I said. Our new C.O., Captain Pulliam, was monitoring our frequency and told us to get off the radio. We had an anxious, but uneventful night. Alpha Company, however, wasn't as lucky. Over half their men were killed or wounded.

Chapter 14

TRIP WIRES AND MINES

Since our unit was now significantly depleted due to casualties, we hoped we would be sent to Cu Chi for a stand down. In the meantime, we continued to operate by working the Michelin Rubber Plantation using tracker dogs. On this particular day, I was walking right flank. As I approached the hedgerow encompassing the rubber trees, I stopped for no particular reason. I heard no "voices," it was just a "gut feeling." I was convinced that a higher power made me do this. I just stood there frozen as my eyes began to scan the area in front of me.

Suddenly I saw it; a green string or wire with hints of red in it. As my eyes followed it, I found an object tied to the tree. I hollered to the rest of the patrol describing the device as a heavy-duty trip flare. Capt. Pulliam said, "That's meant for us," and sent the engineers over. It was a Chinese-Communist (Chicom) grenade. The timer had been removed so when a GI hit the trip wire, which was at neck level, the grenade would explode and decapitate its victim. We blew the grenade and I entered the plantation. As we began patrolling, Capt. Pulliam hollered, "Tell that man to walk faster." He was referring to me. I hollered back, "Tell the Captain that if I'd been walking faster, I would have tripped that booby trap." His response was, "Tell Senka, if he'd walked faster he'd have found it sooner." I felt dispensable.

On one of our patrols, we were walking in the rice paddies. We were anxious because the enemy often booby-trapped the dikes knowing GIs would walk on them rather than through the water. When we reached a large canal, Lt. Mosher told us to walk through it. I told Hank Maul, "Forget that;" we were only about 100 feet from the road. There was a group of South Vietnamese soldiers on the road. They wore clean, tight fitting fatigues and they were laughing at us. We all thought, "Here we are up to our necks in this swamp while they sit out there supposedly guarding that bridge." Hank and I pretended we didn't hear LT. and continued walking towards the road. Suddenly, Lt. Mosher stopped our patrol and gave Hank and me a direct order to cross the canal, which we did. When we got on the road, one of the other men told us that the ARVNS had mined the area in front. Hank and I were walking straight into them. That taught me the meaning of "Blind Obedience." Never again would we question Lt. Mosher.

We began to receive replacements each day. There was no chance that we were going to the rear; we were staying out here in the boonies. One of the replacements came in from LBJ (Long Binh Jail). He strummed his guitar and told me how he had gone to Australia on R&R (Rest and Relaxation) and while there he fell in love with an Australian girl and married her. He spent six months in Australia before he returned to Vietnam and surrendered. It wasn't that he refused to fight. He just did what he wanted rather than following the Army's rules. They put him in jail and none of his time in jail, or in Australia, counted towards his tour of duty. He had now been out of the States for eighteen months and still had to complete his tour, another six months.

I didn't trust this guy for some reason. We seemed to have different value systems. I was not happy to learn that he was assigned to my bunker. That first night I took first watch as I always did. I preferred this so I could do my job then have an uninterrupted sleep. You can imagine my surprise when the Company Commander Ramon Pulliam and the Battalion C.O.

awakened me, a Colonel we'd never seen before. I was told that I'd fallen asleep on bunker watch.

"Bullshit! I pulled the first watch and then woke up this asshole," as I pointed to the replacement from LBJ.

"You have to make sure the guy you woke up is awake," they said.

"I did make sure. As a matter of fact, I chatted with him for awhile."

The next day I was to report to the (CP) Command Post to face an Article 15 hearing. I told Pulliam that this was "bullshit" and that I had a spotless military record. He claimed he knew this and rather than busting me to PFC, he would only forfeit two thirds of my pay for the month. Spec. 4 Perez, our machine gunner, wasn't as lucky. He was there for an Article 15 too. He was a good soldier, often taking the jobs no one else wanted. When I first arrived at the Manchus, Sgt. Steve Laird, a "Shake & Bake" Sergeant new in country, ordered me to carry the machine gun. I refused. Since it had been a year since I worked in my MOS, I did not feel comfortable with the M-60 and I thought me manning the machine gun would jeopardize the lives of my buddies. Perez stepped in and cheerfully agreed to carry the heavy weapon. Laird later tried to make me carry a flamethrower. I'd never even seen one. Captain Winters had rescinded that order.

On this occasion, newly promoted Spec. 4 Perez had gotten drunk and fallen asleep in the grass. Perhaps he needed some escape from the reality of war. Sgt. Laird couldn't see fit to leave him alone, and instead he woke him from a sound sleep and began harassing him. Perez had enough and began swinging at Laird. He then threw the machine gun into the air and it fell onto the ground in several pieces. We let him go until he started to lock and load his M16. Phil Glen then grabbed him and held him, a move that probably saved Steve Laird's life. It wasn't over yet. Before long, a contingent of Puerto Ricans began beating the crap out of Sgt. Laird. He deserved it. On this day, Capt. Pulliam not only took Perez' pay, but busted him back to PFC. He did not deserve to be punished that harshly, but he never complained.

We continued our routine of patrolling, setting up ambushes, and sending out listening posts. Charlie Company was receiving new recruits each day. New letters arrived daily. My Father had finished the harvest for 1968 and everyone was preparing for the Christmas season. Sandy still talked about our future. This was all a fairy tale to me, mundane and insignificant. I was literally fighting to stay alive a day at a time. I hated this place, the weather, the bugs, the people, the smell, everything about it, and I still had a long time ahead of me. I was upset that Danny's unit might be moving out. I enjoyed having him near. Ironically, it was Charlie Company that got orders to move out.

We were going to a position near the Cambodian border near Tay Ninh. It was thirty years later when I learned that Charlie Company and Bravo Company were being set up as decoys – more like sitting ducks. I guess our Commanders felt this was their chance to draw in a large group of North Vietnamese soldiers (NVA) in hopes of killing a bunch of them, even if it meant a few of us would be "killed or maimed." We were obviously expendable. I said goodbye to Danny as we Manchus were told to prepare to move.

We were told to send all unnecessary equipment such as radios, cameras, and personal items to the rear. We were also issued flak jackets that we hadn't worn previously. In retrospect, we should have known that we were being sent into harm's way. We rendezvoused with Bravo Company at a barren location about two clicks (klm) from the Cambodian border.

This was about mid-December. The following days were spent on patrols and digging large deep bunkers. Hank Maul was always near me and we had become close friends. Donnie Culshaw, a muscular seasoned rifleman from Minnesota, worked with me in building our bunker. We spent several days in the blazing sun digging and filling sandbags. We placed steel sheets over the bunker, then put a layer of sandbags over the steel, and eventually dug out the rice paddy dikes and put the earth and grass on top of the sandbags. This not only camouflaged our position, but also provided an unobstructed field of fire on our portion of the perimeter. It was hot, dirty work, but Don and I agreed we'd rather do this for the rest of our tour than engage the enemy. Ironically after all that work, neither Donnie nor I got to use the bunker we built.

63

Chapter 15

MOLE CITY

It was December 22, 1968, and a Christmas truce had been declared. A prisoner exchange was taking place nearby. On this particular morning, Charlie Company was on a pacification mission. We walked through one of the villages with our empty M16s in one hand, our magazines in the other, and our arms were stretched high over our heads. Several of the troops passed out T-shirts with U.S. propaganda printed on them as a gesture of peace and goodwill. Since our new Fire Support Base (FSB) was so isolated, we hadn't received mail or supplies in several days. I noticed our eggs for breakfast were green, supposedly from local gook chickens. We nicknamed our new home "Mole City" because everything was underground.

Trenches connected our bunkers. From the air, it looked like an empty field.

Trench in Mole City

At about 9:00 p.m. on the 22nd, we finally received fresh supplies and mail from a truck convoy. It was wonderful getting Christmas cards from friends and family, even from school kids and strangers. There were cookies from home, and even a miniature artificial Christmas tree that Donnie placed on top of the bunker. We were really happy! SFC. Barrs, a new replacement and a "lifer," stopped by our bunker. A lifer is a career soldier, someone who joined the Army and planned to stay twenty or thirty years until they could retire. He was impressed with the work we had done and thought our bunker, like the others, could survive a direct hit by most anything. Barrs also asked me if I'd ever gotten my Article 15. I hadn't and he winked at me and said, "I won't say anything if you don't."

At about 10:00 p.m., we were given our orders for the evening. Don was going to go out on a night patrol. Evidently, Intelligence suspected enemy activity along the Cambodian border. Phil Glen and Jose Olea would also join the patrol that eventually totaled nine. My instructions were to occupy and defend one of the other bunkers.

I was glad to see Hank Maul in my bunker. Justin Anderson, a tall, blond Swede from Chicago, was also there. I engaged Malcolm True, one of the newest replacements, in conversation. True, who was from Cocoa Beach, Florida, had just arrived along with Jimmy Walker from Red Oak, Oklahoma. The newest "grunt" told me he was married and his wife had just had a baby. He was obviously very much in love and a tape recording from his wife was his constant companion.

At about midnight, the lieutenant told us to get ready – there was going to be a "Turkey Shoot!" We were told that there were a hundred gooks between the patrol and us, and that the patrol couldn't get back in.

We had no idea that 1,500 hardcore NVA soldiers were storming in from Cambodia. Little did we know, we were outnumbered three to one. I was shocked to find out many years later that this had been a suicide mission, and each enemy soldier had his grave marker strapped to his back.

The sky suddenly lit up. It looked like daylight as illumination rounds floated from the sky, dangling from their parachutes. The sky was further brightened as ammo dumps exploded. The four of us began firing our M16s through the narrow slots in our bunker. We blew all our claymore mines, still not fully understanding the hellish nightmare we were about to face. Malcolm True and I climbed out of the bunker and vigorously heaved hand grenades. As we rejoined Hank and Anderson, a grenade suddenly exploded, filling our dark hole with deadly shrapnel. Almost in unison, we screamed, "I'm hit!" We were lucky; none of us were hurt badly. We quickly got into position and laid down a devastating hail of gunfire aimed at the human wave assaulting our position. Hundreds of enemy soldiers targeted our sector of the perimeter and our bunker. Malcolm and I emptied several magazines into them, some within ten feet of us.

Seconds later, a tremendous explosion filled the air. Anderson let out a blood-curdling scream! He was within inches of me. Looking his way, I could see he was dead. My eyeglasses were blown off my face, as was my helmet. Not realizing my right leg was shattered, I instinctively started crawling behind True out of the smoke-filled "hell hole," and into a muddy trench. We found another bunker filled with GIs, many already wounded. A young medic was doing his best to help those most in need. As we barely squeezed through the rear entrance, we suddenly heard a thud in the mud next to me. My brain told me that a hand grenade was going to blow – the "gooks" were inside the wire and engaging us in hand-to-hand combat! Impulsively, I threw myself towards the center of the blackened dungeon.

Following the explosion, there was a deadly silence. Trying desperately to regain my senses, I discovered three of my comrades were still able to fight. One of them was a new replacement that had just arrived in the country. I recall he was from New York City. He was slightly over 5' tall, and he fired a "blooper" (M-79 grenade launcher). Roger Cantrell, also a newcomer, was in good shape, as was Lynn Welker, a respected squad leader from Jonesboro, Arkansas.

Unable to move my lower body, I urged the others to keep firing. Unbelievably, concussion grenades were tossed in; I still remember being hit in the face and hesitating to open my eyes for fear that I was blind. I'll never forget the sudden silence as my eardrums exploded and blood streamed down my face. My lungs and nostrils smelled and felt like the inside of a gun barrel as yet a third grenade exploded, filling my belly with hot steel. As I lay there, I prayed that this would soon end. As I gazed into the area outside of our bunker, the bright light was again visible. The shadow of someone walking in a zombie-like manner appeared. Remarkably, Henry Maul had somehow found me. He crawled into our hole and collapsed by my side. He was somewhat delirious and I urged him to stay quiet. From the corner of my eye, I could see Sgt. Welker climb out of the bunker and into the trenches. The silhouette of him firing his M16 has been etched in my mind for thirty-four years. I remember seeing him hit by small arms fire and rolling past me into the bottom of the bunker. My many attempts to get a response from him were futile. He appeared to be dead.

Some hope filled my head and mind as the gunships approached. As their guns rattled away, the enemy became silent. When the "choppers" departed to resupply, the enemy once again could be seen and heard scurrying among us like deadly rats. At one point, an enemy soldier jumped into my shelter making this probably the only time I was certain I would die. What crazy thoughts were in my mind? Math! As a high school student, I was lousy at it; I absolutely hated it. All I could think was, "If I knew this was going to happen, I wouldn't have worried so much about math."

Slowly, reaching for my weapon and aiming at the gook's heart, I suddenly was painfully aware that the gun barrel was filled with mud. Gently, I placed the weapon beside me, my legs were curled up to protect my genitals and groping the dark, I found a fruitcake tin which I plopped over my head in a desperate attempt to protect myself. Miraculously, no bullets hit me as the "Dink" sprayed the interior of our bunker. How much time had passed? I didn't know. Unconsciousness soon engulfed me.

It was probably a blessing as I later learned enemy soldiers filled my bunker. Apparently I too appeared dead intermingled with the other bodies. I learned that at one point our own troops fired a 90mm bazooka type rifle into my bunker hoping to kill the enemy occupants. They assumed all the Americans were dead in there. Ron Figueroa, one of the Non Coms there that night, described me as a walking miracle.

Chapter 16

GIFT OF LIFE

There was daylight outside when my eyes opened again, but it was completely silent. A different kind of fear came over me. Who won the battle of Mole City? Were the NVA in control? Would I be taken prisoner? How bad were my wounds? The only other person moving was Cantrell. He nonchalantly told me his leg was no good and that he wanted a drink of water. I felt a canteen under my torso so I dug with my fingers until I freed it. I then tossed it to my buddy.

A black mortar Sergeant poked his head into our blackened grave and rejoiced, "There are some Americans alive in here." It was the most beautiful sight I've ever seen. I urged him to get Hank Maul out first because he was hurt worse than me. "You get out first, because you're blocking the entrance. Besides, your friend is dead."

I was flooded with emotion when it became apparent that I was saved. The reality of what had happened these past seven hours struck me like lightning. The realization that most of my buddies were dead caused me to sob uncontrollably. Tears filled my eyes and fell onto my bloodied uniform. I was angry that my buddies and I had to go through this. As the second shot of morphine entered my body, everyone could hear me screaming, "I hate this place! Send me to LBJ (Long Binh Jail), because I refuse to come back!"

The medics who were picking steel out of my gut and leg assured me that I wouldn't have to return. "You're going home," he said. Sgt. Barrs knelt next to me. His skinny hands were shaking violently. "You okay, Hoss?" he asked, as he handed me a cigarette. I welcomed the smoke and sucked the life out of that Winston. Barrs instinctively handed me the whole pack.

The medic said, "Senka, there is only sitting room on this medivac chopper. You can wait for the next one."

"Negative. I can sit, I'm not staying here a moment longer," I replied.

They loaded me on and as we lifted off I could still hear small arms fire. Within a few minutes, I blacked out again.

When I awoke, I was at the 12th Evacuation Hospital along with several dozen other wounded GIs. I spotted Lynn Welker's stretcher and was elated to discover he was alive.

Welker hollered, "You okay, Senka?"

"I'm fine, just surprised to see you Lynn. I thought you were dead." I worried terribly about my buddies.

I spent all day under a covered patio type shelter. Stretchers were lined up all over the place. As I looked around and saw guys with arms and legs blown off, I knew how lucky I was to have survived the massacre at Mole City. I learned later that as a last ditch effort, Capt. Pulliam begged for artillery to be dumped on our own position. The hope was that we Manchus would get into our bunkers and the NVA regulars would be out in the open and cut down by our artillery. It worked and saved our lives. Unfortunately, there were some Manchus maimed by our artillery and were bitter about Ray Pulliam's decision and disagreed with my assessment.

As I laid on my stretcher, the nurses periodically gave me a shot so I'd sleep. Each time I awoke, there would be fewer patients. This was called triage where the worst injuries were treated first. If I remember correctly, I was one of the last to go to surgery. It was nighttime when I awoke in a hospital ward. It was a building with beds lining the floor. It was quiet. The wounded were hooked up to various pieces of lifesaving medical apparatus. My eyes scanned the ward going from bed to bed, patient to patient. My brain was going 200 mph thinking about all that happened to me in the past twenty-four hours.

Intermittently, I would begin to think of what might lie ahead for me. I was mostly contemplating where I was, how I got here, and about my buddies. I was worried about them. Mole City had been a living hell on earth. I prayed my friends had survived. I was enjoying the clean sheets, a real bed, and the opportunity to sleep. I felt moderately safe for the first time since I arrived in Vietnam. The ward was dark and quiet. I was told that it was Christmas Eve and asked if I'd like to go to the mess hall for a Christmas service.

My bed was wheeled out into the cool, evening air. It felt so good breathing fresh air as I was wheeled into the large room filled with patients. It was actually an older nurse, a Colonel, who stayed with me. Christmas Carols were sung. I tried to sing, but soon broke out in a cold sweat. I was too weak and the gray haired Colonel suggested I go back to the ward. It was unbelievable that I could go from being a "strong as iron" combat infantryman to someone too weak to sing.

On Christmas morning, the first sight I saw upon opening my eyes was a young nurse. Normally, the nurses wore combat boots and green fatigues like anyone else, but today she had on a crisp, starched white nurse's uniform including the cap.

She looked over at me and said, "Merry Christmas."

"Merry Christmas. When am I being sent to Japan?"

She assured me that it would be soon, but not today. I worried that maybe I wouldn't go home or perhaps I was afraid the hospital would be hit and I'd be unable to defend myself. I had a cast on up to my hip for my badly shattered leg, my eardrums were both blown out, my belly had an 8-inch hole in it, and the rest of me, from my nose to my toe, was filled with shrapnel.

That afternoon, as I sat in my bed puking from a reaction to the morphine, I saw a gook walking towards me. He was pulling an IV behind him. As our eyes met, I began screaming verbal abuses and profanity at him. He represented the bastards that had done this to my unit and me. I'll never forget the sad look in his eyes. I began to weep. What the hell was happening to me? For all I knew, this young Vietnamese could have been a South Vietnamese soldier, or an innocent civilian. I just saw his dark skin, slanted eyes, and assumed he was the enemy. I sensed that I was not the same; I just didn't know how much I had changed.

I don't remember much about Christmas day except that I was anxious to leave. I wondered if my folks knew about my fate. When a GI went into a combat zone, he was asked if he wanted his family notified if he was ever wounded, I opted not to do that. I was afraid that if I received a "scratch" they'd notify my parents and upset them. I didn't wish to put them through more worry than they already had. Knowing the Army, I figured that if I was seriously wounded, they would disregard my wishes and contact my folks anyhow.

That Christmas afternoon I had a visitor. His name was Richard Deacon. He was a well-known character actor who played Mel on the *Dick Van Dyke Show*. Richard was a tall, baldheaded man who wore thick, black glasses. He sat on my bed and chatted. I was surprised that he was originally from Binghamton, N.Y., though he hadn't been back there in years. I told Richard that Sandy was from Endwell, N.Y., which was just west of Binghamton. I think it was wonderful that celebrities took time to visit us Vets on Christmas Day, and I think of that day in 1968 whenever I see a rerun of one of Richard's TV shows.

Chapter 17

TENDER CARE AND CARELESS TREATMENT

On December 26, 1968, I was put on a stretcher and loaded onto a bus. Our stretchers were stacked along the sides of the bus on hooks. I could see out the windows that were covered with screen mesh to protect us from hand grenades. We rode through the city until we reached the Air Force Hospital near the airport. We were to spend a day or two there until we were ready to be flown to Japan. This was a beautiful hospital! The Air Force sure lived better than the Army. Our food was brought to us on stainless steel covered dishes.

The Air Force medics were a different breed as well. One of them offered me a bedpan. I had not had a need for one in several days.

"I'm not using that."

"Well, Senka," he said, "you can't walk so you have no choice."

"Watch me. I'll get to the bathroom if I have to crawl."

He placed a wheelchair next to my bed and I grabbed the overhead bar and dropped into the wheelchair. The bathroom was designed for guys like me so I could use the rails to get from the chair onto the toilet. This is the first real toilet I'd seen in a long time. It sure beat the usual hole in the ground with an ammo box covering it. We would sit on that in full view of other grunts and even Vietnamese passersby. Talk about no modesty! I sat in this sparkling, white, bathroom for quite awhile just flushing the toilet and listening to the water. I was like a kid with a new toy.

I returned to my bed where I met a gorgeous, coffee-colored nurse who was waiting for me. She was a Captain and she was tall and beautiful. She asked if I would like my hair washed.

I eagerly replied, "I have half the dirt in Vietnam in my hair."

After the enjoyable wash, she said, "John, can I do anything else for you?"

"Would you mind writing a letter to my folks for me?" I told her what to say and she wrote it and mailed it for me. I was ready to leave for Japan the next day.

The Air Force medics played loud music throughout the ward mostly from the new musicals, "Hair" and "Jesus Christ Superstar." In order to amuse themselves, they took advantage of my helpless condition and began placing wooden matches between my toes that were protruding from my cast. They then threatened to light them! I didn't know whether to laugh or cry. "Damn you bastards," I would shout. Then I'd start laughing, seeing the humor in my situation. Each time I laughed, my belly wound would cause me to cry out in pain. It was a real effort not to laugh and the medics got a real kick out of it.

The next morning we were being prepared to transfer to the 106 General Hospital in Yokohama, Japan. In preparation for the five-hour flight on a C141, those of us with casts had to have them split in half. It had something to do with the air pressure. Aaron Burrell was my new companion who had traveled with me on the bus. He had been wounded in the arm and was ambulatory. I enjoyed his company because he always had a smile and a story to tell.

The guy in front of me was from Oklahoma and had a right arm that was barely attached. He told me that the morning he had been wounded, he continued firing his machine gun determined to see his newly-born baby. In the end, he literally grasped his arm to keep it from falling off. When his turn came to get prepared for the flight, the Specialist 5, a "lifer" with a week remaining in the Army before retirement, began manhandling him. The GI said nothing, but I could not stand watching this. "Hey asshole, quit being so rough with him. He damn near lost that arm," I yelled toward the disrespectful medic. The Spec. 5 glared at me.

"Are you a Marine?"

"No," I shot back.

"Well you act like a Marine."

He did seem to treat the kid from Oklahoma more carefully after that. When my turn came, he made certain my cast was screwed up (my knee did not fit where the knee was supposed to fit into the cast and it felt like my knee was being rubbed raw). I guess he got even.

The C141 cargo plane was redesigned for use as an in-flight hospital. Row upon row of stretchers were stacked, one over the other. There were seats for those that could walk. The huge plane taxied down the runway and finally took to the sky. In a few minutes they announced that we had flown out of Vietnam air space. A feeling of relief came over us — we finally felt safe. We were on the first leg of our journey back to the world and as such, we all shouted a big hurrah!

Chapter 18

BACK TO THE REAL WORLD

At the 106th General, we were assigned to our various wards. Japanese civilian ladies worked on the ward filling water pitchers, cleaning and so forth. The Japanese Company Sony gave each of us patients a new transistor radio. The days were long and boring. We had to get up by 7:00 a.m. to clean up for the day. I looked forward to evenings when Aaron Burrell would sit next to my bed and tell me stories. We smoked and took our pain pills together. Aaron had been raised in a boy's home near Peoria, Illinois. Apparently, some guy named Pop-something was the head guy at the home. Aaron's eyes lit up when he talked about Pop, the same as most boys would when talking about their dads. Aaron was married, had a child, and was excited about going back to Illinois. As he rambled on, the pain pill "kicked in" and my arms seemed to float.

On New Year's Eve, the hospital added a bottle of beer to our medicine tray. On New Year's Day, Aaron left for the United States and I was prepared for additional surgery on my leg and stomach. Two new patients were brought into the beds next to me. One was an older guy who had served in Korea, but wanted to get in on the action during Vietnam. He joined the Navy and served on a river patrol boat. He was here now with part of his thigh blown away. They actually brought him his skin in a jar and he'd lay it over his wound for transplantation.

In the opposite bed was a quiet "old" guy with a pure white crew cut. I thought he was some lifer Staff Sgt. or something. Pretty soon I noticed high-ranking people visiting him. I soon discovered this was Command Sgt. Major Daniel J. Mulcahey who was the top enlisted man in the 11th Armored Cavalry. The 11[th]s Commander was Colonel Patton, son of General George Patton. Apparently, Col. Patton was similar to his famous father right down to the pearl handled pistols he wore. He had his helicopter land amidst a firefight and in the process a gook popped out of a "spider hole" and shot the Sgt. Major. Dan responded by killing the gook. He had previously been awarded a Silver Star for an earlier action. It is unbelievable that this man who was too young for World War II and who never got sent to Korea, now as a Command Sgt. Major got shot in Vietnam. Dan and I became friends and our friendship still exists thirty-four years later. He was from Maine and had that "backwoods" kind of common sense. I think us younger guys amused him, yet he had genuine respect for us.

Shortly after surgery, my abdomen became infected. The front of my stomach swelled like a bulge in an inner tube and turned dark blue. That night two of the doctors doing their residency in the Army walked through. I stopped them and showed them my belly. One turned to the other and in an obvious Southern drawl said, "I'll teach you how to lance that tomorrow," and walked away. These two young men in blue jeans looked more like farm boys than doctors. As I wheeled myself around the ward, I felt something wet in my convalescents. I glanced down, my bulge had ruptured, and ugly looking puss ran down my belly. The nurse looked at my wound and said that the doctor would look at that in the morning.

When morning arrived, both doctors came directly to my bed. They looked disappointed when they saw my belly. The older doctor turned to his understudy and said, "I guess old Senka beat us to it." He then said to me, "I'm not going to stitch this. I'll let it heal from the inside out, but I will clean it." I turned my head and stared at Sgt. Major Mulcahey who was staring back at me. As they began working on me, it began to hurt like hell. I grabbed the rails of my bed and as I did, I noticed a gruesome look on Sgt. Major Mulcahey's face. When these young physicians were done, they turned to one another and said, "Old Senku seemed to think that hurt." After they were gone, I questioned Dan, "Were they serious that it was not supposed to hurt?" Dan said, "My God, they cut your skin with a pair of scissors then stuffed you full of gauze."

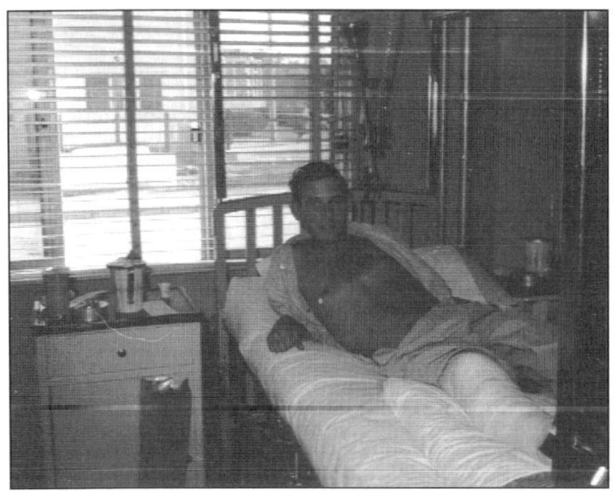

John at 106 General Hospital, Yokahama, Japan

By now my folks had received the letter I sent. As it turned out, the Army honored my request and never notified them of my being wounded. When the letter arrived, Mom realized that it was not my handwriting and called Dad who was in the potato warehouse. She was in tears when he walked into the kitchen. Even though he was not a drinking man, he downed a shot of brandy before he opened the envelope. They were relieved when they knew I was okay. They had expected the worst. Mom later related to me that Dad had a tear in his eye, and even though he seldom expressed his emotions, he said, "He's my son, too. I've raised him since he was a baby."

After that they called Sandy who was visiting my sister. The Red Cross was contacted and they told Sandy that a phone call to me would be arranged. When the call came, I spoke to

Mom and Dad and assured them I was okay. Sandy then spoke to me. She was cheerful and excited. Something was not right with me because I had no interest in speaking to her. Instead of being excited, I was concerned with the cost of the call. I could relate to nothing she was saying. Something was wrong with me. I could only imagine how disappointed she must have been.

A few days later my friend, the Sgt. Major, was being sent to the States to the Army Hospital at Ft. Devens, Massachusetts. I hoped I'd see him again someday. I began to grow restless as I began to heal physically. I was ready to go home to the United States and inquired each day as to when I'd be sent home. They asked me where I wanted to go and I told them that there was a Veterans Hospital in Bath, N.Y., which was thirty minutes from Arkport. The Naval Hospital St. Albans in Long Island would be fine or the Army Hospital at Valley Forge, Pennsylvania would be okay, too. I was told these military hospitals were filled to capacity, and that I was not eligible to use the VA Hospital because I was still on active duty.

Several days passed when I suggested that I'd be willing to go to Ft. Devens. Ron Strobel always spoke highly of the place and maybe Dan Mulcahey was still there. Ft. Devens was about six or seven hours from home, but it was fine with me. I had been at the 106 General for almost a month when I was told I was going home. I would be flown to Walter Reed Army Hospital in Maryland and then put on a smaller plane for the flight to Ft. Devens.

Two days later I was loaded on the aircraft for the long flight back to the States. Like most of the other men on the plane, I spent the entire flight lying on my back on a stretcher. We landed at Walter Reed Hospital in the dark of night. I was half asleep when a colonel placed an object in my hand, a small medallion from the Veterans of Foreign Wars organization. It read, "Welcome Home Your Country is Grateful." Inside Walter Reed, the Red Cross paid for each GI to call home. Being back on U.S. soil was a feeling beyond description. Early the next morning I was carried to a small plane that was sporadically landing throughout the Northeastern part of the US leaving broken bodies and broken men along the way.

Chapter 19

TWO VICTIMS OF WAR

It was the middle of January 1969. It was cold and there was snow covering the ground when I arrived at Logan Airport in Boston, which was quite a change from the weather in South Vietnam. I was packed into the back of an ambulance and driven to Ft. Devens. The hospital was a wooden structure built during Word War II. It was an exact square; the center was like an atrium. The four halls making up the square were so long that you could walk until you walked out of sight.

I was placed in a bed on the surgical ward. Everyone on this ward required nursing care. The soldier to my right was a guy named Joe who had been there for over a year. When I met him, he was in a full body cast. He confided to me that he had seen guys come and go and he couldn't stand being here. His left leg was badly injured and would always be 6 inches shorter than the other. He asked the doctors to amputate it and fit him with a prosthetic leg. I guess the medical community felt a flesh and blood leg, even a crippled one, was better than no leg. Joe wasn't so sure because he received letters from former patients who were back in civilian life bowling and dancing on their artificial limb.

This was a time of reflection for me. I was still reliving and reflecting on my combat tour and the horrors of December 22nd at Mole City. I sent a letter to Jay Schmid, my buddy from boot camp, to let him know I had been wounded. Each time the "Stars and Stripes", the Army newspaper, was delivered we would search the list of KIA (Killed in Action) and WIA (Wounded in Action). I was hoping not to see any familiar names, but all too often we found the names of buddies from our old unit, from boot camp, or from AIT. Sometimes we'd discover the name of an NCO or officer who had trained us. It was from this list that the deaths of Justin Anderson, Hank Maul, Phil Glenn, Malcolm True and many, many others were confirmed.

In Vietnam, soldiers had no opportunity to mourn the death of a friend or to grieve. They were with you one minute, healthy and alive, and dead the next. Their bodies would be placed in bags and taken away while the rest of us were expected to continue as normal. Here in the hospital it was different. After learning of a friend's death, I would return to my bed and think and wonder why I was spared while other sons, fathers, and husbands died. I never saw the Vets cry. It's not that they were in shock. They were more emotionally numb. In combat, they never had the opportunity to grieve for their buddies. People died and we just moved on with our daily routines and missions. Patients tried to console one another, and often we shared our stories. I had never seen such bonding, love, and caring since that time in the hospital, other than in Vietnam itself.

Time at the hospital ward went slowly. Many volunteer groups visited us or came to entertain us with music and song. They even went shopping for us. I had no clothes or uniforms, just the blue convalescents. I asked a volunteer if she would buy me a pair of slacks and a sweater so I'd have them when I needed them. In Nam, I used to dream about buying a pair of desert boots, a comfortable ankle high shoe made of buckskin and lined with furry material. I knew that as soon as I got out of the hospital, I'd find a pair even though I could only wear one. Every evening there was a pretty, blonde-haired, Spec. 5 medic who would offer to give us a massage. There were very few of us who would turn her down and I for one looked forward to them. It was something to look forward to at the end of the day, a temporary release from hospital routine.

A few weeks after arriving here, I got a letter from Mom and Dad saying they would be driving to Massachusetts to see me and they were bringing my fiancée Sandy. I was nervous about seeing them, but not sure why. I knew there would be questions about my tour and knew they wouldn't understand. How do you explain to someone about walking miles in the hot sun, how it felt not to sleep, about how it feels to be hungry or thirsty, or how it feels to see your best friend blown into bits and pieces? You can't, and I didn't try.

The day of their visit arrived and I woke early to clean up. I pulled on my new slacks, splitting one leg so it would fit over my cast. I put on the sweater and my Army dress shoes. I had been given crutches the day before so now I could get around easier than I could with my wheelchair. I paced the long hospital corridors on my crutches anxiously awaiting their arrival. I saw a civilian walking towards me. Could that be Dad? Yes, it had to be. He wore a dress hat as men his age often did. I approached him on my crutches and shook his hand. We were both nervous. He directed me towards the main lobby where Mom and Sandy waited anxiously. When I got there, Mom broke down and cried. She was thanking God for saving me as she hugged me. Sandy waited for her turn patiently. I turned and embraced her, but something was not right.

I couldn't look at her or make eye contact. For her, the waiting was over. The man she loved was home safe and sound. For me, my ordeal was just beginning. I knew I wasn't the same as I was before I left for Vietnam. I didn't smile as much. I was more serious and always thinking — not only about the war, but also about my future. I was jumpy, nervous, and I easily became angry. Mom, Dad, and Sandy would soon find that out. Dad wanted to get a motel, but I told them I had arranged for rooms at the Post guesthouse.

I had to get my bag and asked my Father to walk to the ward with me. I could tell he was uncomfortable seeing so many young men with missing limbs or paralyzed by spinal injuries. I introduced my Dad to Joe who repeated his story about his long stay at Devens. We met Mom and Sandy and drove to the guesthouse and then to a restaurant for lunch. Waitresses would inquire about my leg cast, thinking I'd gotten hurt skiing. Mom would proudly tell how her son had been wounded in combat. Sandy and I spoke very little and Mom would nudge me to hold Sandy's hand. It was pretty obvious something was wrong. After lunch I asked my Dad if he'd take me to a shoe store so I could buy the desert boots that I'd been wanting for so long. Mom again repeated my story to the shoe salesman.

Back at the guesthouse, Dad asked me what happened at Mole City. As I slowly conveyed the events of that evening, my voice would crack and tears would swell in my eyes. Talking about Vietnam was not easy and I realized this wasn't something I would do often in the future. We had a great dinner that evening although I could not eat as much as normal. I had lost thirty-five pounds since Mole City and my stomach had shrunk. During dinner, I sat next to my fiancée, but made no eye contact and showed no signs of affection, not even holding her hand. Her normally sunny disposition was gone. She had a scared, bewildered look on her face. She was wondering what the hell was wrong with me. After dinner, we drove to the guesthouse, which was no more than some private rooms in a wooden, World War II billet. The furniture was Army issue right down to the beds. Having lived in a hole in the ground for so long, I thought it was great, but I should have realized most people would find the accommodations less than acceptable.

Mom and Dad went to their room and Sandy and I shared a room. As soon as she was away from my folks, she allowed her tears to flow.

"What's wrong?" she asked.

"I honestly don't know Sandy, but whatever it is, it's me, not you."

I was numb and I couldn't express my emotions. I knew I was breaking her heart and I hated myself for it, but I couldn't do anything about it. We stayed up most of the night talking. We both realized that I had changed and consequently our relationship had too. They packed up for home the next day. What should have been a happy reunion was not. Many years later Sandy told me the ride back to New York was uncomfortable. Mom made excuses for me and was sympathetic towards Sandy. My Father's only comment was about my shoes, something about the one shoe not being worn and how it was too bad I couldn't have split them with some guy who needed a right shoe.

I returned to my life on the ward. I saw the doctors each day and got treatment for my leg, belly, ears, and other shrapnel wounds. My hope was to be able to get a convalescent leave soon. When I saw the doctor later that week, he told me I could go home for thirty days. I asked if my steel sutures would be removed before I went on leave. He said, "No, we'll remove them when you return."

Chapter 20

ANXIOUS RETURN HOME

I was so excited about leaving! I was sent to supply to get new dress uniforms so I could fly home. The Army had sent a Bronze Star and Army Commendation Medal for "heroism" to my home. In addition, I had earned the coveted Combat Infantryman's Badge, Purple Heart, and various Vietnam Service medals. My new uniform was quite decorated. I rode the bus to Logan Airport in Boston. As I waited for my flight, I saw a group of soldiers probably right out of boot camp. They were staring at me, particularly at my injury and at my chest full of ribbons. As I sat there, I was glad my military service was ending and hoped these new soldiers would never have to experience the horrors of "Mole City."

Mohawk Airlines was the only carrier flying to Western New York and, because they had a monopoly, they did not offer military rates. I had to pay the full fare. It didn't matter because I would soon be home. I flew into the Monroe County Airport in Rochester. It was a blessing that I had no baggage because it would have been impossible to handle with crutches.

As I sat down in the terminal waiting for Dad, I recognized Nate Kaplan, one of my friends from college. Nate was the one who actually arranged for me to meet Sandy. I had no interest in seeing him, let alone talk to him. The truth was, I suddenly resented him. I was angry that my buddies and I had to go to hell and back while guys like Kaplan were probably enjoying the good life. He was a draft dodger, which was a presumption on my part. Kaplan spotted me, but I could tell he wasn't certain the soldier was the same wild, college kid he knew. I sat down and lit a cigarette. Before long Nate sat down across from me. He peeked around his newspaper. He must have seen my nametag and he probably wondered what was wrong with me, and why I wasn't talking. To this day, I don't know why I acted that way, but it only confirmed what I already knew, something was not right with John Senka.

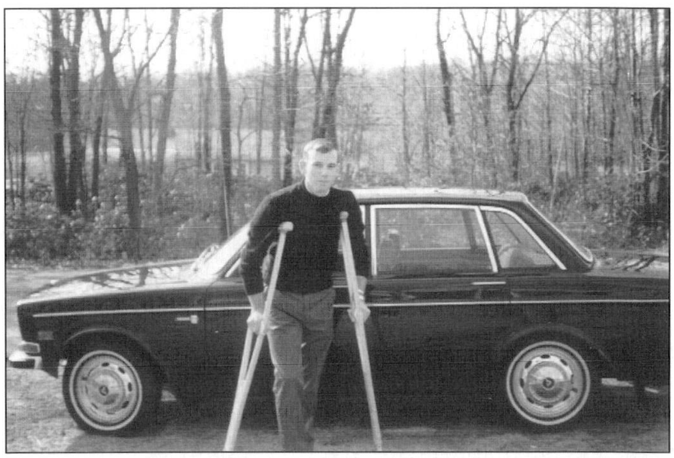

On convalescent leave

Dad's blue, "Olds" pulled into the parking lot and I hobbled out of the terminal leaving Nate Kaplan to ponder the question of what happened to Senka. Driving through the winter wonderland of upstate New York was a pleasure. It was interesting to see how things had changed. Before long, we were home in Arkport. My brothers, Joey and Bobby, were excited to see me, but they were somewhat shy. I often contemplate that if I'd been killed, I'd only be a vague memory to them. I know this from talking to younger siblings of some of the men who died at Mole City.

I had now been back in the states about a month and it was wonderful being back home, safe and sound. I looked forward to sleeping in my own bed and eating some home cooking. Unfortunately, I hadn't slept well since returning to the States. The slightest noise would bring me out of a sound sleep, the seven-hour battle at Mole City played over and over in my mind like a non-stop movie.

Then there was the episode that took place early one morning on the surgical ward. Unbeknownst to me, the hospital chaplain, a priest, came by the beds of the Catholic patients to give absolution and to serve communion. It was dark, and I had been sleeping when I suddenly sat up and threw a fist at the priest, just grazing his head. I felt terrible and apologized over and over. I was experiencing what I later learned was something called hyper-vigilance. This is a symptom of Post-Traumatic Stress where a person is ready for fight or for flight, a basic animal instinct.

My first morning home, my Mother brought me a couple eggs for breakfast. It turned out to be more than my stomach could handle. After that, she would scramble one egg and about thirty minutes later she'd bring the other. I was anxious to go downtown to see some of the village citizens. Most of my friends were in the service, and those who had avoided service would be working so I decided to go to the barbershop. Bing Howe, the local barber, had a son serving in Vietnam with the Marine Corps. A World War II Vet himself, he gave the military men that were home on leave free haircuts. He also had a large display in the shop with all the "Village sons'" pictures posted on them. Under each picture was the man's military address and colored stars indicating those killed, wounded, or in Vietnam. It was a thoughtful gesture of appreciation, one that I have never forgotten.

On this day, my Mother had to help me exit the rear seat of her car. As soon as Bing saw me through the shop window, he ran out and welcomed me home and invited me into the barbershop. Sitting in the shop gave me the opportunity to see lots of men in the Village. Some of the elderly gents may not have known who I was, but Bing made a point of telling them. I later learned that there had been several news clips in the local newspapers about my being wounded in action. The article referred to my Army Commendation Medal with V Device for "heroism." I felt uncomfortable with that reference. I was no hero, but rather an ordinary "grunt" that happened to be in the wrong place at the wrong time. The real heroes were guys like True, Maul, Culshaw, Briggs, and a list that encompasses more than 58,000.

I could tell that some of the customers in the barbershop were uncomfortable seeing me; they didn't know what to say. After a few hours, I became restless and decided I would walk to John Hubric's house, my friend from Ft. Campbell, to see his folks. I departed on my crutches. Having gone less than a block, I became exhausted and lightheaded. I found myself in the front of Janice Ludwig's home. Janice was the mother of my childhood friend, Freddy Kemp. Freddy was killed at Quang Tri province while I was in boot camp. I became extremely anxious and developed a cold sweat. "Oh God, get me out of here," I thought. I didn't want Mrs. Ludwig to see me. I was afraid to see her, what would I say? I realized that what I was really experiencing was guilt. I felt guilty for having come home; knowing her son did not. Mustering all the strength I could, I moved my crutches forward as fast as I could.

By the time I had visited with the Hubrics, I was exhausted and "Big John" Hubric had to drive me home. I retreated to the safety and privacy of home. This first day was almost more than I could handle. The word was out now that I was back, so many of my friends stopped by the house. Very few of them asked questions. Either they were afraid to ask or didn't really understand where I had been or what I had done in Vietnam. They were not interested in hanging around my house and it was great to have them take me out for rides and to visit our old "watering holes." One thing that struck me as peculiar was that while my friends ordered beers, I had "graduated" to bourbon. Often I would drink as many glasses of bourbon as they did beer. The more I drank, the less I thought about Mole City, Cu Chi, the Hobo Woods, about Hank, Andy, Glen, True and the others. Until I went to sleep and the movie would start again.

I would stay out late and sleep late. My Mother cooked all my favorite foods. Sandy called me from her home and wanted me to visit her family. I wasn't interested in leaving Arkport so she asked to visit me for the weekend. I didn't want to see her, but didn't know why. "Sure, come over this weekend," I said. Mom became visibly upset with my behavior, especially where Sandy was concerned.

People asked me what my plans were now that I was back. I hadn't thought about it. I was trying to enjoy the moment. I had felt dead and now I was reborn. I appreciated the little things other people took for granted, such as cold water when I needed it, a hot bath, flushing toilets, being able to walk through the farm without fear of tripping a booby trap, and clean clothes and a clean bed. But now it was different. The future was not important to me; I wanted to enjoy myself now.

Chapter 21

WAR REMINDERS

My leave went quickly and before I knew it, I was scheduled to report back to Ft. Devens. When I arrived, there were several surprises awaiting me. Sgt. Major Mulcahey was now Post Sgt. Major and he continued to visit me. All the hospital staff was wondering what my connection to Dan was. They also moved me from the surgical ward to the Medical Hold Company. This was an entire ward for patients who only saw the doctors at weekly clinics. There were no medical personnel on the floor, only the C.O. (Commanding Officer), Lt. Maloney, a very compassionate and pleasant man, and a couple of clerks. They had one of the patients, a Sgt. First Class lifer, who was an Airborne and Combat medic, oversee the ward. He was a short guy with raven black hair and a matching mustache with dark piercing eyes and a deep baritone voice. He never smiled.

I moved my small bag of personal items to one of the beds on the ward and I met some of the GIs on the floor. They had a couple of formations each day, but basically we were free to come and go as we pleased. Most of the men were from New England and many had automobiles on post. I soon learned the main in hospital hangout was the Red Cross Lounge, a canteen with vending machines that supplied everything from cigarettes to soup to sandwiches. My first night back I stayed at the Lounge until 10 p.m. before returning to the ward to go to sleep.

About 2 a.m., all the lights in the unit came on and I could hear yelling and screaming. What the hell was going on? Four or five guys were returning from an evening of drinking. We could hear glass breaking in the latrine area and holes being kicked in the sheetrock walls. I was scared since I knew I couldn't get out of bed very easily. The next thing I saw was a wheelchair being tossed across the floor followed by two combat Vets fighting within a few feet of me. I saw the fellow on the bottom reach for a solid glass ashtray and begin smashing it into the head of his adversary. Blood was starting to cover the floor. Before too long the Military Police were there and the ruckus was over. As I tried to fall back to sleep, I wondered if this was normal for this ward. It was also obvious that I wasn't the only one with a problem.

The next morning, we learned that the one soldier received 110 stitches in his head and that both men were being shipped to Walter Reed that day. I learned long ago that whenever I got to a new unit, it was best to keep my mouth shut and my ears open. It gave me the opportunity to learn about the other guys. I lounged around the ward most of the day. We had amputees, double amputees, leg amputees, arm amputees, and men in wheelchairs due to permanent nerve damage. One young Lieutenant had been hit in the shoulder by a rocket-propelled grenade (RPG) that had not exploded, fortunately for him or he would have disintegrated.

There were some nice Vets in the Medical Hold Company. I took an immediate dislike to the SFC with the black hair. I didn't trust him. He treated the other patients as if they were trainees in boot camp rather than respected combat Veterans. That evening I joined my friends at the Red Cross Lounge for coffee and some smokes and chatter. About 10 p.m., we decided to turn in for the night and started back to the ward. What we saw next was beyond belief. There were patients loitering in the hallway and an amputee was on the floor polishing the metal threshold with Brasso and a toothbrush! A sign hung on the wall to "Keep Out." "What the hell is going on?" I asked. I was told Sgt. Jones had them cleaning the ward and the floor was drying. Sure enough, there was that black haired "prick" standing in the middle of the floor on his crutches as if he owned the place. I flew into a rage like I'd never done before. I told the guys to go to bed and for the amputee to stop working because he had earned the right not to put up with this bullshit. I told Sgt. Jones I was going to bed. His face turned red as he screamed in that deep baritone voice, "The hell you are soldier." I said, "F--k you," and started across towards my bed, my crutches leaving imprints on the wet floor. He started towards me swinging his crutch at me. I stopped and did the same; you could hear wood against wood echo through the ward. It was over. I hopped into bed and hollered to the others that they were crazy to let him push them around. I then fell asleep.

I made a point the following day to learn more about that "jerk" Sgt. Jones. He had been in the Army about ten or twelve years and was indeed a highly decorated soldier. I envied him for one reason; his medals, unlike mine, were for saving lives not for taking them. He was not in here for combat wounds however. He had been in a motorcycle accident at Ft. Bragg and his passenger, another soldier, had been killed. He was awaiting a court martial back at Ft. Bragg. I decided to keep this information to myself, at least for the time being.

One of the clerks came out to the porch that adjoined the ward. Many of us would sunbathe out there. "Senka, I have a letter for you," as he handed it to me. I could see it was the letter that I sent to Jay Schmid letting him know I had been wounded. I was puzzled until I saw the red stamp mark "addressee deceased 12/14/68 we regret your letter could not be delivered." I stared at the envelope for what seemed like hours not believing that Jay had been killed one week prior to the "Mole City" battle. "Thanks," I said as I quietly shuffled back to my bed.

I couldn't cry; I just laid there thinking about Schmid. He was the one who convinced me to stay in the infantry rather than apply to a military school. Jay was the one who said, "I'll take my chances in Vietnam before I spend another day in the Army." His poor mother, he was the only son in the Schmid "clan." I wondered how many more of my letters would come back. I sensed someone was watching me from a distance. It was SFC Jones. He asked what was wrong and I told him. He actually appeared compassionate. As he returned to his bed, I could hear him telling the other men about the bad news I had received. Maybe Jones wasn't so bad after all – maybe.

Local Fraternal and Veterans organizations had social events for us hospitalized Veterans. One event in particular stands out in my mind. The Sons of Italy had a spaghetti dinner/dance at their club in Boston. Our entire Ward was driven there in private vehicles. I was in a car driven by the Catholic Chaplain. We all looked forward to an enjoyable evening away from the hospital. When we arrived, we were shocked to discover there were other guests there to join the disabled Vietnam Vets. The other guests were people with cerebral palsy. I'm not sure what the thinking was on the part of our hosts, perhaps to let us see that there were folks worse off than we were.

In any case, it had the reverse effect. Some of the men, who were permanently crippled, threw themselves into the free liquor. Even soldiers like myself lost our appetites and drank excessively. We had nothing in common with these people and as sympathetic as we were to their affliction, it was demoralizing to us. On the return trip, one of the guys began a public confession to the Chaplain. He not only confessed to being obviously drunk, but also told the priest he was using drugs. Before we arrived back at the post, the guy puked in the Chaplain's car. We were all embarrassed, but the priest took it all in stride and the Vet promised to clean his car in the morning.

Drugs were used and abused by the patients. Darvon was distributed like candy. Some of the men were users before coming into the Army, however, some may have become addicted to pain medications as a result of their wounds. One weekend PFC Brill stayed on the Ward. He had served in the Army in the 1950's. A Judge gave him a choice to either go to prison or enlist so he enlisted. We never knew what he had done to warrant this sentence. One hot Saturday afternoon, he walked out to where I was sunbathing and vomited. He was obviously intoxicated and on drugs. He passed out on the lawn still wearing his dress green uniform. I couldn't move him so he lay there for hours.

On Friday we were scheduled to report to the weekly clinic to have our wounds checked. I quickly learned that you often would see a different physician each week and it was easy to get additional leave time.

As the young Captain looked at my leg he said, "Son, do you know you still have stitches in your leg?"

"Yes Sir, I do. Where the hell are they?" I asked.

Only about an eighth of an inch of steel stuck out above the flesh. You could feel it by running your hand over it.

"They should have taken them out before you went on leave. We could leave them in," he joked.

"Great, leave them in!"

He laughed, "Sorry, I can't."

"Oh by the way, Doc," I asked. "Is there any chance I could get a convalescent leave?"

"Haven't you had a leave yet?"

"Yes Sir, I have, but it's been awhile and I'm really just waiting for this bone to heal."

"OK Senka, I'll give you two weeks leave starting tomorrow." He grabbed some pliers, grasped what was protruding and gave a mighty pull that did the trick.

SHADOWS OF WAR

I got my bags together and made arrangements for a flight. I didn't tell anyone I was coming home and decided I'd hitch hike the sixty plus miles home from the Rocherter Airport. A lady picked me up in the terminal driveway and drove me to Wayland, N.Y. A soldier on crutches was pretty sure of getting a ride quickly. The owner of a gas station where I bought gas as a kid saw me and drove me right to my folk's front door. I surprised Mom and then discarded my olive green uniform in favor of my favorite blue jeans and sweater. I made some calls to let my friends know I was back. I hated being at the mercy of others for rides and to help me get around. I was eating better now and started to gain back some of the thirty-five pounds I had lost.

My friend Eddie, who had some kind of plush job in Vietnam, was now discharged and had been home for more than six months, but was still not ready to go to work. He chauffeured me and we'd hit the American Legion in the afternoons. One day a car driven by a cute blonde pulled up next to him and the two of them spoke.

"Welcome home, John."

"Thank you."

"How does it feel to be home?"

"Great."

When she drove away, I asked Ed, "Who the hell was that?" He told me that it was Cathy.

"Are you shitting me? She was just a kid. I'd always liked her Dad. How old is she?"

"Eighteen," Ed replied, "A senior ready to graduate in June."

"What the hell is wrong with me?" I thought. I'm engaged to Sandy. I can't be thinking about other girls.

We drove to the Arkport Inn to visit our favorite bartender, "Beef Stillman." "Beef" was a large, quiet man who genuinely seemed to like the young people that frequented the bar. The bar was empty except for three men in the corner. One was "Batch," a local bum who supposedly disliked the Army so much that he made himself a promise that he'd loaf one year for every day he served. His sidekick was a black man who worked in some of the produce warehouses, and then there was Ray, a milkman who, when not delivering milk, was drunk. The bartender welcomed me home and shook my hand.

After a few drinks, Ray, one of the three patrons confronted me: "I know you think you're a hero. My brother was killed at Anzio Beach. I know what a real hero is." His words were like daggers in my heart. "What the hell is this about?" I thought. I hadn't said or done anything. I never even mentioned Vietnam. I finally told Ray I was sorry about his brother and started to explain that war is war, period. It doesn't matter if it was a World War, a "police conflict," or "military action" when you had a fierce enemy trying to kill you, it's all the same. The trio wasn't listening; they had their own agenda. I finally said, "F--k you," and hobbled out to Ed's car. "Take me home Eddie." "Is this what I'm going to being doing, defending my actions in Vietnam to the ignorant?" I thought. I had to get away so I asked my Mom to drive me to Endwell to visit Sandy. Naturally she wanted to see me spend time with Sandy. Spending the weekend there was relaxing for the most part. Sandy lived in a modest home shared by her mom, dad and grandmother. Her dad was in charge of maintenance at the high school and her mom worked in the library. Her Grandma, who I liked very much, was retired from the Endicott-Johnson shoe factory. Her mom was somewhat overbearing, but they were good, God-fearing people.

Sandy was a pretty girl and she loved me with all her heart. I felt guilty about how I was treating her. She didn't deserve it. We had a chance to talk and be alone. I learned that while I was gone, she had decided she would accept me in whatever physical condition I returned. If I were blind, paralyzed, an amputee, whatever, she would stay by me. I knew that these were not just words, she meant it. Naturally when I heard that, I felt even worse for the way I was acting, not being the loving, affectionate, caring fiancé that I wanted to be.

Sandy and her mother were pressing me for answers about my future plans, which made me uncomfortable. It was now Spring and I hadn't been scheduled to leave Nam until October. "No, there would not be an early wedding," I told her. I wasn't even sure I wanted to be married in the autumn as we had planned. Everything was happening too fast. The Vietnam Vet often was in the jungle fighting "Charlie" one day and two or three days later back home. We Vets who were wounded had weeks to "decompress," but also had other issues to deal with. By the time the weekend was over, I knew I had to get out of there so her father drove me home. It began to seem like I could only spend so much time with people in various situations before I would feel the world closing in on me. I had to get away.

Back home my Mom wanted to play twenty questions with me. When was I getting married? Where would I work? Had I thought about where I would live? Those were the serious questions. Then there were the really annoying ones like where are you going? Who are you hanging out with? What time did you get in? I was looking forward to getting back to Ft. Devens with my Vet buddies. It was April of 1969. Ft. Devens Hospital Medical Hold Company was the only place where I really felt comfortable.

HEALING BODY — WOUNDED MIND

When I arrived back at the Medical Hold Company, the guys were glad to see me. My friend Clark had bought a new Corvette and had it parked outside. The men started to let their hair grow longer and with the sun shining more, we all spent much of the day tanning our combat hardened bodies. With more cars available, we started going out at night. We'd often go to Pettelli's Pizza to eat and drink drafts. The pizza was fantastic! We'd also go to Fitchburg. Fitchburg was a few miles away and had a club with bands playing and lots of girls.

It was really a pretty good life! I made my weekly visit to the clinic and was told my leg was "bowing." They were going to correct it, but then decided not to for some reason I never knew. Today my leg is a half-inch shorter and, after thirty years, it has affected my hip, back, and skeletal system. My other wounds were healing well. Soon they would shorten my cast and put a heel on it so I could walk without the crutches. We continued our daily ritual of cleaning up, having breakfast, and then sunbathing and going out at night depending on our finances. The weekends were lonely because most of the Vets were from New England and went home. I was often the only occupant of this huge ward. It began to get warm on the ward and the only relief was a huge floor fan. When the guys were gone, I'd face it directly at my bed to cool me off, and blow the mosquitoes off of my body.

I received a call from my friend Vince Mahany. "Tyler" had spent six years in the Navy as a submariner. His folks moved to Arkport from Maine. I met him while I was in college when he used to visit his folks while on leave. We became good friends and I even attended his wedding in New London, Connecticut in 1966. Ty and his wife invited me to their home in New London. I jumped at the chance to get out of Ft. Devens for the weekend and appreciated them driving down to get me and bringing me back. Tyler was a few years older than I was and I respected him enough to discuss my personal problems, particularly the pressure I was feeling about marriage. He understood completely.

He drove me back to Ft. Devens and to the ward that was still empty because the men hadn't returned from leave. He looked at the place and said, "I hate leaving you in this dump." He felt strongly that Veterans deserved more than this. Tyler and I stayed in touch and I always appreciated him caring enough to spend time with me while I was going through my recuperation at the Army hospital.

That Monday at clinic, a shorter cast with a heel replaced my lengthy cast. I no longer needed crutches. The following night a bunch of the fellows were going to Fitchburg. What a group we were. Vets in casts, on crutches and in wheelchairs! Sgt. Jones was with us. By now, we had become accustomed to him. In Fitchburg some guy was asking Sgt. Jones about our group. He explained that we were combat disabled Vets and that he himself had stepped on a land mine. That kind of pissed me off and I told him that I knew how he messed up his leg and it wasn't from a land mine. While we were sitting and drinking, I noticed several Vietnamese women at an adjoining table. I couldn't take my eyes off of them, my face turned flush and I was angry. I didn't know why. Maybe they were wives of GIs. Why should these "gooks" be here having a good time while Hank, Andy, Glen, True and Schmid were dead?

Looking back at this period of my life, I experienced many strange feelings and emotions, which I have come to understand. I am not sure if I have reconciled myself to these feelings. It angered me that so many young lives were lost. We'll never know how some of our best and brightest young people could have contributed to humanity. Many of our strong, vibrant warriors had their lives forever changed. They were crippled, maimed, blinded; others lost their minds. Families were divided, loves lost, personalities gone.

On top of all of this, no one seemed to care. Most people didn't even know what was happening. Those that did, not only had no empathy for Vietnam Veterans, but also considered us losers. I had always been pretty jovial and easy going. Now I was serious about life, I trusted few people, I got angry easily, and I got close to very few people, only those I respected. Seeing these women brought Vietnam back into my head and I wondered about all the Manchus in Charlie Company. What were they doing tonight while I was here partying? I ordered more bourbon in an attempt to deaden my mental anguish.

Before I knew it the weekend would be here and the place would be empty. Lt. Maloney called me to his office.

"Senka," he said, "General Westmoreland will be on the post this weekend. We'd like to have him present some of the Vietnam Veterans with their medals. If you'll stay here this weekend, I'll give you a three day pass whenever you ask."

"No problem, Sir," I replied, because I wasn't planning to go anywhere. I was told to get into my dress greens and wait. Saturday arrived and I put on my uniform and waited, and waited, and waited some more. It was almost dark when someone told me I could change my clothes and leave. Apparently "Westy" didn't have time to see me. Lt. Maloney apologized later, but it wasn't his fault.

At the clinic, I saw Captain Brock who I had seen several times previously. He was a nice man, just doing his time. He had been drafted like so many others. The tibia was healing, but I still had to be there for a while. "Sir, may I have a convalescent leave?" I explained that I lived in New York and couldn't go home weekends like the others. "No problem, Senka, take twenty days leave." I packed a duffel bag and carried it to the bus the next morning. It was heavy and not easy to carry with my walking cast. Three of us exited the bus terminal in Boston. We had to catch another bus to Logan Airport. The bus terminal was about 1,000 feet away with unbelievable traffic between us. Most people could walk or run across, but in our condition it was impossible. We stopped a cab and explained that we were disabled Vietnam combat Veterans and we had to get across the street. This cabbie said, "Welcome home boys, this country should do all they can for you guys." My first thought was that he'd take us across for nothing. What would it cost for a ride across the street?

"$4 apiece."

"$4? We just have to go there." I pointed at the terminal.

"Well, I can't drive straight there. I have to go around the Square."

I really wanted to walk but knew I'd never make it. Reluctantly I said, "OK." I thought, "Welcome Home all right!"

Chapter 24

EXPLOSIVE REALITIES

It was now late May and it was great being home. Dad had started planting his crop. The weather was beautiful. Trees were in blossom, birds were singing, and I had spring fever. It was great to be alive. I spoke to my Dad about buying a car. I guess he felt I deserved one because he agreed to co-sign for my loan. I found a sharp, 1968 Pontiac Firebird that I liked, but couldn't drive because of my leg.I needed an automatic transmission. We found a 1967 Mustang Fastback at Charlie Wilkins' in Hornell. The owner's wife was driving it. I loved the dark green color, the chrome scavenger pipes and the deep, mellow, glass pack mufflers. This was the first good car I'd ever bought and the first time I borrowed money. I then purchased insurance and was no longer at the mercy of others to get around. The car was a "head turner." I hadn't been to any movies lately, but I was told it was the duplicate of the car Steve McQueen drove in the movie "Bullet." Sandy came down that weekend and we waxed the car.

By now, some of my Army buddies were home after completing their hitches. Charlie Schwarz was back from Germany working at Eastman Kodak in Rochester, Ron Strobel was back from Nam and was working at Goodyear and John and Bev Hubric were back from Ft. Campbell, Kentucky and were living in Buffalo while John enrolled at the University of Buffalo. We had a big party that weekend, cooking steaks in my Mom and Dad's basement family room. We all got pretty drunk. Mom was glad to see me with these old friends because John and Ron were married and Charlie had a girlfriend. She assumed this would bring Sandy and I closer.

I was starting to realize that I had to start thinking about the future. I had financial obligations now and in a few months I'd be out of the hospital. The Army gave you the choice of completing your two-year hitch or taking a discharge if you had less than six months remaining on your tour after leaving the hospital. I was certain I'd get out. If I had my way I'd take off across the country, perhaps visiting the families of the boys killed with me in Nam. That was a "pipe dream," as I had no money. Oh well, I figured something would work out.

I continued to enjoy my time home. I spent time with Cathy, even went to Loon Lake with Mary Nolan, the nursing student. One night, I was by myself and ran into three girls from high school. They were all one or two years older than I was and extremely attractive. We shared a booth at the Arkport Inn and drank several rounds of drinks together. One of the girls, Janie had just gotten divorced. Lonni and Shelli were still married, but Lonni was not happy with her marriage. I shared my apprehension about marriage and all three advised against it. The four of us went bar hopping and before the night was over, Lonni kissed me passionately before going home. I took Shelli home and it was early in the morning before I returned Janie to her ex-mother-in-law's house. Perhaps Vietnam Vets were objects of interest to others, possibly even curiosities.

When I returned home, it was about 4 a.m. and the house was locked. "What the hell is going on," I thought. I flew into a rage and began ringing the bell and banging on the door. Within seconds the lights were on and my Mom answered the door. She began questioning me as to where I'd been and why I was so late. I tore into a rage like nothing she had ever seen. "It's none of your DAMN business where I've been or who I've been with.

Why the hell are you locking me out? I'm not a child anymore.
Do you know where I've been? I've been to hell and back. I
lived in filth, I've killed and I've seen my buddies blown to hell.
Please don't ever lock this door again or I'll break it in."

Mom cried as I staggered past her and into my bed. I
spent the rest of my time at home seeing Lonni and Cathy. I
continued to ponder my future and my relationship with Sandy.
Bourbon continued to be my relief from the pressures of life and
the images of Vietnam and Mole City that continued to fill my
sleep time. The situation at home worsened. Dad said very little.
I knew he was not enjoying this. Mom had discovered I was
seeing Lonni. Apparently my sister had been snooping around
and heard the rumors.

This was against everything sacred in my Mom's eyes.
She also knew about Cathy and I believe, if the circumstances
had been different, she would have encouraged my relationship
with her. Finally one day in a heat of anger, I told my Mom that I
was not getting married and I was ending the relationship with
Sandy. Mom, with tears in her eyes, fired back that if I did that,
she was no longer my Mother! Her words hit me in the heart. I
was mortally wounded. I could not speak. She continued to tell
me about the "hell" that I put them through. I was confused and
wondered, where do these people think I've been? On a cruise in
sunny, Southeast Asia? I wished it could be that easy. Now I'm
back and ready to live happily ever after? I went to the phone
and told Sandy it was over. She was devastated and told me to
come down. "No. I'm returning to the Fort, back where it was
safe, back where I could think, back with my own kind, back
with my grunt buddies who understood." I packed the Mustang
and started my six-hour journey.

Chapter 25

PUSHED FROM THE
SAFE HARBOR

The next morning I laid outside in a lawn chair as one of the patients came out.

"Senka, I have a job for you."

"A what," I said.

He explained that 1ˢᵗ Sgt. Carter had put him in charge of a detail to assign us to various hospital wards. "Bullshit," I said, but I couldn't get angry with him; he was a nice guy just doing what he was told. I was upset that the Army would even think of putting us Vets to work. Hadn't we done enough? We gave our blood, limbs, and more for our country. This was an insult. Nonetheless, I decided to go. I was assigned to a dependents ward. The patients were mainly wives of servicemen. My job was to fill water pitchers at each patient's bed. This was not something I enjoyed.

On Tuesday, I was scheduled for clinic. Dr. Brock told me the leg was healed and they would remove the cast. It was now late May of 1968 and I knew the leg would be weak from months of immobility. It felt great having it taken off and I started physical therapy and began to learn to walk again and to rebuild the muscles. I appreciated how fortunate I was as I shared the therapy room with amputees, paraplegics, and others. On my days off I was put to work on the wards until I had enough. I walked off the ward and told the guy in charge to "go to hell." 1st Sgt. Carter called me into his office and asked what this was all about. I told him the truth. I thought it was ridiculous that the Army was making disabled combat Veterans, who were still hospitalized, work. I then told him standing on my feet caused my ankle to swell. He took one look and excused me from any further work details.

I now had time to think about all that had happened since my return. My life felt like such a mess. This should have been a happy time, but it wasn't. I worried about my future. During this time, I would visit Sgt. Major Mulcahey at his nice home on the post. I told Dan about the pressures I was encountering at home. Dan asked me if I'd ever considered making a career out of the Army. I hadn't really. He asked if I'd like to go to Officers Candidate School. Looking back on these days, I'm certain that whatever I wanted within the military, Dan would have helped me get it. I seriously contemplated re-enlisting, figuring that with my record I'd move up quickly. More realistically, I was looking for a safe haven.

On Friday afternoon, Lt. Maloney approached me. He was being temporarily transferred to Indian Gap, Pennsylvania. He had five Sgt. E-5 promotions available and asked if I wanted one. I told him I'd think about it. It didn't make a big difference now, unless I decided to stay in the Army. At the Red Cross lounge, all the men were talking about the promotions. I listened and realized some of these boys planned to make the Army a career and really wanted and needed these stripes. In my heart, I knew that staying in the Army was not in the cards for me. I thanked Lt. Maloney for the offer, but suggested he give my stripes to SP/4 Roski. Roski wanted to go to Military Police School and make the Army his career and Maloney agreed.

That same afternoon Lt. Maloney, 1st Sgt. Carter, and the Colonel in charge of the hospital came on to the ward. They called us to attention and into formation. We wondered what on earth was happening. The Colonel then called for me to come "front and center." He then read several sets of orders for various medals, including the one for "Heroism," and presented them to me. He ordered me to face the formation and hollered "Present Arms" as a ward full of my peers, dressed in their blue convalescent uniforms, saluted me. I was humbled and was more honored than if General William Westmoreland himself had done the honors. I had not expected any formal recognition, or public acknowledgment. I don't think I wanted any.

When it happened, I was emotionally touched that it was from my peers, my brother Vets. It meant that I had earned their respect and that was important to me. I also learned an important lesson that has followed me throughout my life. You must earn respect. Respect moves and motivates men. Authority doesn't. Before Lt. Maloney left, he asked me if I'd like to move into his apartment off base and share expenses with his roommate, the clerk at Medical Hold Company. I moved out of the hospital the following weekend. I still had to report in each day and make afternoon formations. On one of those afternoons as I walked through the hospital, I saw an office marked "psychologist." Perhaps I needed help. After all, it was obvious that the way I reacted to Sandy was not normal for me. My excessive use of alcohol and my moments of rage were also out of character.

As I walked towards the office I thought, "This is crazy. Here I am, surrounded by amputees, paraplegics, the blind, and other severely disabled Vets, and I'm going to complain that 'I don't feel the same.' Quit complaining and move on with your life, and be glad you are in one piece."

I was writing to Sandy and talking to her on the phone. She felt that if I were calling off our marriage then I should be man enough to visit her folks and tell them. As hard as this would be, I agreed to do so on my next leave. She also informed me that she was considering leaving her nursing job to join the airlines as a stewardess, most likely leaving the upstate New York area. I had a lot to deal with and it was time to go home again.

Dr. Brock told me I'd be ready to leave soon and that thought scared me. This was my safe harbor. It was where I fit in and belonged. I wasn't like other people. Although I was only twenty-one-years old, I felt I'd lived a lifetime already. I was tired and old.

Chapter 26

IN THE WORLD WITHOUT CRUTCHES

It was the first of June when I took my last convalescent leave. The weather in upstate New York was gorgeous, the grass was green, the trees were in blossom, and the birds were everywhere. My first stop was Endwell. I told Mr. and Mrs. Nikl the wedding was off. Mrs. Nikl was not happy and asked why. I had no good answer and that was the truth. The previous autumn, the thought of marrying Sandy was like a dream come true. That was before Vietnam. What changed me so drastically? Was it the horrible living conditions I'd experienced as a grunt? Was it the heartache I felt from seeing small children eating out of dumps and living in filth? Was it from seeing young American boys blown to shreds or crippled for life? Was it from being forced to kill or maim an enemy in order to survive? Or was it from months of thinking of only myself in an effort to survive. I was terrified that I was no longer capable of loving another human being.

Sandy accepted my decision though. Her mother thought she was crazy and said that if it was her, she'd give me back the engagement ring. Thus began the first incident to undermine my relationship with her folks. I felt better because the pressure was off. If I decided to get married, it would be my choice, and not due to "heat" from my Mother or Sandy's mom. Sandy and I enjoyed our time together and we even visited some of her friends. Her friend Carol's husband, Wayne, worked for Prudential Insurance and whenever we visited them, he and his friends would be talking about how great the insurance business was. I remembered in college the professors often spoke of students who were successful insurance salesmen. Even though I did poorly in college, my grades in sales and business courses were excellent. My Dad's insurance agent for his farm was highly successful and prosperous. Our Metropolitan Life agent, Bob Powell, was a happy-go-lucky guy. He was always whistling and had a new car every other year. I thought I should give the insurance business a try.

When I got back to Arkport, I began to think more seriously about my plans for the future. I really wanted to stay in the area in which I was raised. Not necessarily Arkport, but a small town. I drove to Hornell and met with Jim McGlaughlin, the New York State Veterans counselor. Jim and I hit it off immediately and it was apparent he would help me in any way he could. He informed me that as a 40% disabled Veteran I was entitled to rehabilitation in the form of four years of a free college education and I would be paid $350 a month on which to live while I was in college. He emphasized that this was not a gift, but that I had earned it with my blood. I thanked Jim and told him I'd give it serious consideration. My next stop was the prudential office where I met with Ed Story. His first question was, "What's wrong with your leg, you limp?" I briefly explained that I was wounded in South Vietnam and was still in the Army. Although Ed was pleasant he made a point in telling me that he had a file full of applicants and that my disability was a consideration as it could worsen and Prudential could end up putting me on disability retirement. He did invite me back when I was discharged and told me the starting salary for an agent was $135 per week.

I was already discovering what some of the men at Ft. Devens had told me, "fifty cents and all your medals will buy you a cup of coffee." I could actually go to college full time and get as much from Uncle Sam for a living allowance as I could working. This would require some thought. My biggest fear was that if I went to college, I'd fall into my old pattern of partying, raising hell and so forth. The one thing I had now was some respect and some control.

Small rural towns are not like the cities where Vietnam Veterans were afraid to wear their uniforms for fear of confrontations. No one ever spit on me in Arkport. I could see the respect in people's eyes and their demeanor when they spoke to me. I knew it would take only one incident, one bad judgment on my part to lose that respect. I never let that happen. I owed that to Hank, Andy, Glen, True, Schmid, Dave Briggs and all my other friends who died in Nam. I carried a heavy burden, as did all Vietnam Veterans to make the most of the life they were spared. We owed that to the 58,000 men and women who didn't have the chance to return home. Yes, I had problems. I was not the same. I had little in common with my non-vet friends, but I had a dream, and a mission, to put this Vietnam War behind me, to put it in a footlocker and lock it, and block it from my mind. It was over and it was time to move on. And that was what I did. In retrospect, perhaps that was a mistake. You cannot bury a troubled soul.

Chapter 27

CROSSING THE DIVIDE

My trip back to Massachusetts was in mid-June. Ft. Devens was a beautiful spot with its scenic lake in the center and manicured lawns. I looked forward to spending the summer here and touring New England. Tom Falzoi from Arkport lived in Worcester, Massachusetts, a short distance from the post. Tom was a few years older than I was, and, as a child, he had been my Boy Scout Den Leader. Tom had spent eight years in the Army and was discharged with the rank of Captain. He was kind enough to spend time with me while I was at Ft. Devens, for which I will always be grateful. I spent weekends at his apartment and we'd visit all the local clubs.

On the 19th of June, I reported to the weekly clinic. On this day, I saw a new physician, someone I had not seen around the hospital. He asked me what my problem was. He was abrupt and did not smile. I knew in an instant that he and I weren't going to be friends.

"My problem," I replied, somewhat sarcastically, "is that some gooks f   d me up with some hand grenades "

"Well, you are ready to return to duty." His tone of voice pissed me off.

"I'm never going back to duty."

"Well, then you can take your discharge." I glared at the cocky son of a bitch.

"How long do you think I've been in the hospital?"

"I don't know."

"I was wounded December 22, 1968, so I've been hospitalized six months."

"Well, in civilian life, people can't afford to take that much time off from work."

"Look," I said trying to reason with him, "I still limp and my ankle is stiff. It's going to be difficult for me to get a job in this condition. I'd like to spend the summer here and get discharged in September. By then my leg will be totally healed." I never gave thought to the emotional healing. He got a smirk on his face, and said, "Senka, you either go back to duty or take your discharge." I said, "I'll take my discharge," as I walked away. At that moment, I felt like knocking him on his ass, but didn't.

I found Dr. Brock and told him the story. He said that he was sorry there was nothing he could do. "Who the hell is that guy, Doc.? I've never seen him around here." Dr. Brock shook his head and informed me that he was a reservist doing his two weeks active summer duty! Obviously, this reserve doctor knew nothing about the Army or about the War.

I spent the rest of the day filling out forms, taking a physical, and going from one building to the other. Hospital Headquarters told me to report to building "A" at noon the next day and to have my dress green uniform on. "Must I wear my uniform?" "Yes, it is a privilege to be discharged in uniform. If you had a dishonorable discharge you would not be allowed to wear your dress greens." I went from bed to bed saying goodbye to this menagerie of "gimps" who had become my brothers, my family. I would miss this old hospital ward, which was a safe haven and my home for so long. I could only wonder what life had in store for me.

The next morning I showered, put on my uniform and drove to building "A" to receive my discharge and paycheck for the month. My emotions were mixed. This was the day every soldier waits for thinking it will never come. This day closed a chapter in my life, a chapter that marked me for life. Vietnam was the experience of my life that defined the man that I would become. Thirty years later I discovered the chapter never closed. As I went through the line, I was told that my money had been sent to my home address. "Well, that's terrific. I don't have any money other then the $2 in my pocket." The clerk handed me a $20 bill and said, "Here, this is your travel pay from here to New York." I hoped that that would buy enough gas to make it home. An old Sergeant I met at the NCO Club handed me a large manila envelope. "Senka, here are your hospital records. You aren't supposed to have these, but take them anyway because the Army has a way of losing things. Who knows, twenty years from now you may need them."

It was my turn next. I snapped a salute to the Major and said, "Specialist Senka reporting for discharge, Sir." He returned the salute and said, "Thank you for your honorable service to your country and the United States Army," and handed me my discharge orders. It was over on June 20, 1969. I was a civilian once again. I was only twenty-one-years old.

Chapter 28

ENTERING A CAREER

On the way home, I picked up two hitchhikers. They were "hippies" and seemed frightened of my uniform. Hell I had nothing against "long hairs." In some ways, I envied their carefree lifestyle. They were heading west to California. I took them to the Canandaigua exit of the New York State Thruway and bid them a safe journey.

I decided to stop by my sister's house to tell them I was a free man. Jean's husband Mike was a great guy who I enjoyed spending time with. She also had two kids that I enjoyed visiting. Jean and I were getting along okay, of course, that was probably because I had been gone for the past two years. After spending the night with them, I drove to Arkport the next morning. I took off my dress greens and began my search for a job. I had only one suit so I donned it and drove to the Prudential Office. As I limped towards the front door, I got scared and I didn't know why. This should be a piece of cake compared to the infantry. I returned to my car without going in. I'll drive by the Metropolitan Insurance office. Mom had mentioned to our agent Bob Powell that I was looking for work. Bob, who knew me since I was a young child, offered to help if he could. I later learned that Bob who was a quiet, private man had been a Flying Tiger pilot in World War II. Perhaps he knew what I was going through and would be willing to help.

As I drove into the parking lot, Bob spotted me and waved. If he had not done that, I don't know if I'd have entered the building. He introduced me to Andy Murphy, one of the managers. "Murph" and I hit it off at once and he arranged for me to take a series of aptitude tests. Three days later he called and said the job was mine if I wanted it. I was elated and decided to take the job in Cohocton, N.Y. Cohocton was a small rural community similar to Arkport. I wanted to go where people didn't know me.

Vietnam always seemed to surface, like when I met Dick Roche, one of the other managers, a fine man and experienced agent. He went out of his way to help me on many occasions during the early years of my career. I soon learned that Dick's son, Jon, had been killed in Vietnam about the time I was wounded. He had been a heroic helicopter pilot. This information really hurt me, although I tried not to show it. I sensed sadness in Dick. Did he sense the guilt I felt each time that we were together? The guilt I felt for being home, enjoying life, working, wearing clean clothes, sleeping in a clean bed. In a word, the guilt of being *alive*.

At this point, I severed ties with Cathy, Lonni, Mary and anyone else. My goal was this job and I pursued it as aggressively as I would a combat mission in Vietnam. My relationship with Sandy was getting better now that I was home. She was still two hours away, but we talked often and spent weekends together. It was not the same as it was before Vietnam, but nothing was the same. Not my relationship with my family or friends – everything was different. The reason everything was different was because I was different. I had experienced what others could not even imagine. I didn't even try to explain it to anyone.

War is unexplainable; it has to be experienced. Working twelve-hour days was the norm for me and I had no problem doing this. "At least no one is shooting at me," I thought. I enjoyed selling insurance and competing not only with the thirty salesmen in my office, but also all the other agents out there from other companies. I buried myself in my work and put Vietnam behind me. At least I thought I did.

I wasn't sure I was ready for marriage, but I wasn't sure I wanted to lose Sandy either. I wanted to be like other people. I wanted a wife and children. When I was on combat missions, I would think how sad it would be if I died never having left anyone behind to carry on the Senka name. My Father, although he never was able to see me, still left someone behind to carry on the legacy. I almost lost that opportunity. I was smart enough to realize that the past was the past. No one cared what my buddies or I did in Vietnam, our sacrifices didn't matter. What we did or did not accomplish in life was up to each of us. That's the way life is. The burden was on our shoulders. Fair? Who knows, who ever said life was going to be fair?

Many of my non-veteran friends were living the good life. Many had good jobs with gas companies, phone companies, and other large industries that became available while the rest of us were serving in the Armed Forces. The War itself brought prosperity on the homefront. This was nothing new since it was also true with all past wars. Vets such as myself were entering the "rat race" late and had some catching up to do. I was determined not only to catch up, but to also to get my "piece of the pie." I owed it to my Father who never lived to fulfill his dreams. I owed it to all my buddies who would never fulfill their dreams, and I owed it to Sandy and our future children. Most of all, I owed it to myself. I had earned the right to a good life. I knew it would not be easy This was a competitive "dog eat dog" business. The pressures and quotas were enormous. If you didn't sell, you didn't eat. It was as simple as that.

Chapter 29

LOVE CONQUERS

In September of 1969, I was sent to New York City for formal training for two weeks. Before departing, I told Sandy I wanted to get married and to make the plans for November. Dad would be up to his neck with the harvest until then. We always planned our lives around the farm. I enjoyed the training school at Met Life Headquarters and met some wonderful young men. Several, I soon discovered, were Vietnam combat Vets like myself. There were many nights we would wander into Greenwich Village or Harlem in the evening. Our instructors would warn us against doing this and we'd look at one another and laugh. What danger was there in sightseeing in New York City compared to our patrols in Nam?

When I completed my training, I returned to Hornell. Andy Murphy welcomed me back and told me that Ray Benza, our district manager was back to work from disability and he'd like to meet me. I liked Ray very much. He was an Italian and a devout Catholic. He had worked hard and was enjoying the rewards of his position. He told me that my new supervisor would be starting next week. His name was Tim Conway, a young twenty-four year old guy, married, with one child. He had been a hotshot salesman in Elmira, N.Y. and was recently promoted to staff manager. I had appreciated the help "Murph" provided me those first few weeks, and will always be grateful to him for giving me the opportunity. I was willing to work with anyone, and welcomed the chance to learn more about the insurance business.

Tim Conway arrived on Monday and he seemed like a pleasant young man. He had a new suit on each day and I often felt embarrassed that I still only had one suit to wear. I knew I had to buy some clothes, but I was now paying room and board, the car payment, plus the high cost of gasoline as I was on the road a lot. I was also saving money to buy a mobile home for Sandy and myself. It was now October and our wedding was scheduled for November 15, 1969. Although I was Roman Catholic, Sandy's family wanted us to be married in the Methodist Church in Endwell. My folks were probably not happy with this, but said nothing. They probably felt that getting us married was the main goal, and where we married was secondary.

Sandy and I bought a beautiful mobile home and found a private lot in Cohocton for it. Dad agreed to enclose the undercarriage and build stairs for the front and rear. I asked my brother-in-law Mike to be my best man. Then I asked Chuck Schwarz, Ron Strobel, John Hubric, and Bucky Roosa to be my ushers. Even though Joey and Bobby, my brothers, were young, we included them in the wedding party. Sandy included Jean as a bridesmaid, along with her daughter, Lisa, as the flower girl. We invited most of the employees at work. It was a wonderful Slovak wedding held at the Moose Club. My Dad paid for an open bar, but I made a point not to drink at the reception. I didn't want to get drunk and lose control of my emotions. I did, however, have a "screwdriver" before the ceremony in order to calm my nerves. We had a great wedding and Sandy was a beautiful bride.

Sandy and John, wedding day
November 15, 1969

As we prepared to leave, I picked her up in my arms and literally ran out with her. There was no time or money for a honeymoon so we spent the night at the Travel Lodge in Syracuse and drove to our new home on Monday. We spent Monday getting settled into our home and establishing bank accounts at the local bank.

Chapter 30

THE MOLE CITY GUEST

On Tuesday, I went back to work. Tim had planned to work with me and that was fine, but I hadn't expected him to eat dinner with Sandy and me for the next two weeks. I later learned that the company paid him for dinners on their expense account. This spoke volumes about the man's character. We sold lots of insurance over the next two weeks using his high-pressure tactics to close the sales. He was more concerned about hitting quotas than doing what was right for the client. This wasn't the way I wanted to do business. I was relieved when our assignment was over. At least I could enjoy dinner with my bride. Hard work didn't bother me. I liked the work and enjoyed meeting new people. Cohocton was a nice community.

Sandy was able to get a job as a nurse at the Veterans Hospital in Bath. Our neighbor and landlord, Harvey Young, worked there so she was able to ride to work with three or four others in the community. Although I worked twelve to fourteen hour days, Sandy never complained. I know it had to be hard for her being alone in a new community. Harvey's wife Betty became a close friend and was like a mother to her. Our biggest problem was my drinking. I wouldn't touch a drink while I was working, but weekends were different. I got a job at the Arkport Legion on Saturdays, thinking the extra cash would help us, and that I might meet new sales prospects. Unfortunately, after my shift was completed, I'd move to the other side of the bar and drink up whatever money I earned that day. One evening I was so intoxicated I barely made it home because my car "spun out" into a field. Sandy was frantic with worry. We had a terrible fight over it and I went into my now familiar rage. As usual I would awake the next day remorseful for my actions. Sandy wanted me to quit the bartending job. She was right, so I quit.

Our first Christmas together was fast approaching and the season was festive. We had started to make friends and were invited to a party in Arkport with some of my school friends. We decided to go even though we knew Mike and my sister Jean would be there. We had a nice time, but I drank too much. Sandy wasn't happy with me and at the end of the evening, she drove me to my parent's home. When we got there, Jean and Mike had already arrived. Jean was telling my Mom how intoxicated I was, and embellished the fact that I had danced with some of the other female guests. This was like my childhood all over. She would do or say whatever she could to discredit me in the eyes of my Mother. I felt that all-too-familiar rage take over, and began cursing at her. Sandy tried to calm me down. I walked out of the room as everyone stared in disbelief at how I had acted. Suddenly it hit me like a ton of bricks.

This was December 22, 1969, the first anniversary of Mole City. I began to weep. Sandy ran to my side. "Why did they die? I should be back in Vietnam with my friends. I tried to save them, but I couldn't." I then told her something I'd never told anyone. It involved my buddy Hank. While Hank lay by my side in the bunker, I placed my hand on his head to comfort him and a portion of his skull was gone, my fingers entered the interior of his head. Sandy held me tight.

My "performance" that night confirmed to us that something was seriously wrong. At least that's what I thought. I shouldn't have gone into a rage and then lost control of my emotions like I did. I swore that no one would ever see me like this again. The sad part was that whenever we celebrated a holiday at Mom and Dad's home, it would result in a confrontation between my sister and me that would spoil the spirit of the day. Since I hadn't been home the past two Thanksgivings or the last Christmas, I wanted to spend Christmas with Mom and Dad, and we did.

PREGNANCY AND DEBITS

As 1970 began, I had been with Metropolitan five full months. The new sales year began and I would be competing for the full, new year. The quotas were increased significantly and the "old timers" were bitching about it. Knowing nothing about quotas was an advantage for me. All I knew was you sell or you don't eat. These weren't quotas to me — they were missions. In combat, you accomplish your mission or you don't survive. I was convinced of one thing: that I was a survivor.

In February of 1970, Sandy surprised us by announcing that she was pregnant. As excited as I was, I was also scared. Life was moving too fast! It had been less than five years since high school graduation and so much had happened! Responsibility for a wife, going into debt, and now a baby. All of this made me more determined to hit quotas, to make my "mission" successful. Tim Conway spent a lot of time with me. The older men disliked him so he concentrated on another new guy he had hired and me.

Sandy's pregnancy was difficult, she was sick most of the time in the early days. Since we only had one car, there were times that I would have to pick her up at the VA Hospital. It was

Thursday afternoon, the only day I was required to report to the District Office. Conway had a sales meeting and individual conferences in the morning. Usually by noon the salesmen would be returning to their homes. I decided to stay and work. My debit had not been serviced for almost a year prior to my being hired so many clients were behind in their payments. The agent had to complete a lengthy form at the end of each month for each of these accounts. I had just completed sixty-five of these and had writer's cramp, but at least they were done.

I slid them through a designated slot and then called Sandy. She was ill and wondered why I was late. I explained what I'd been doing and told her I was on my way. As I put on my jacket and picked up my debit book, Tim appeared.

"Where do you think you're going?" he said.

"I'm going to pick my wife up at work."

"Did you complete the lapse forms?"

"Yes, I turned them in."

Suddenly he pulls them out of the folder and says, "You forgot to put page numbers on some of these." It was a trivial oversight.

"Oh, I'll do that Monday. I have to get Sandy at work," I replied.

"You aren't going anyplace until these are done."

That all-too-familiar rage returned. "Look Conway, this isn't the Army. My wife is sick, I'm already late and I'm leaving."

"No you aren't."

"Watch me," I yelled.

"You're fired."

"Fired? For what?"

"For insubordination," he screamed.

"F--k you, Tim," and as I walked out he grabbed my debit book. I drove to the Vet Hospital and told Sandy I thought I was fired. I didn't care because I'd been to hell and back and I wasn't taking any of that punk's shit. One of the more experienced salesmen, Stan Sager, told me that he couldn't fire me. "As long as you don't steal from the company or have an affair with one of your clients, it would take an act of God to terminate you." This was just the first of many confrontations between Tim and me. I seriously considered quitting, but I wasn't a quitter, I was a survivor. This asshole wasn't going to ruin my career.

When I started this job, I had no idea how much money people earned. Dad never talked about his income on the farm and the most I earned in the Army was a $165 a month as an E-4 with combat pay. I was pretty naïve about the cost of living, raising a child and so forth. Pete Gath, a personable agent a few years older than me, told me that $10,000 a year was a good income. I decided that would be my goal. The job was enjoyable, except for the days that I had to report to Tim or the days that he'd work with me. He still had the habit of hanging around until Sandy invited him to eat with us. Working twelve to fourteen hour days became a way of life by now. My performance was good, almost as good as some of the "top dogs" in the office. These men had been with the company fifteen or twenty years and they were all World War II Vets. I respected them very much and in time grew to love them like surrogate fathers.

Chapter 32

BIRTH, DEATH, AND CAREER BLIPS

In October of 1970, Sandy gave birth to our daughter Debbie. We were thrilled! The baby was beautiful like Sandy. As I stood in the hospital nursery grinning at my daughter, I felt someone watching me. It was Conway with a briefcase in hand.

"Hi Tim, what's up?"

"Congratulations," he said. "I heard you were in town. Would you mind going over some lapses with me?" he asked.

"Tim, I'm here to see Sandy and the baby. Never mind, sure, we'll grab a chair in the waiting room." If I'd thought my boss was a jerk before, this eliminated any doubt. We finished our business and he left.

On our first wedding anniversary, there were three of us at home. Sandy and Debbie went to sleep and I celebrated with a bottle of champagne. My first full year in the business, I out sold two thirds of the office and couldn't wait to start the new sales year. In 1971, the company had doubled the sales quota. I wanted to hit the Honor Club Level so Sandy and I could get invited to one of the conventions.

Sandy had her hands full with a baby to care for. We decided if there was any way to do so, we'd keep her home to care for our child. My Mom had always been there for us and it was important that our children be home with their mom, rather than with a babysitter. If I worked hard, I could earn enough so that Sandy wouldn't have to go back to the Veterans Hospital. That was much different from many of our friends, where both parents worked.

The people at Metropolitan Life became like family to us. The older guys would share facts about their business and personal lives to help us. They tried to keep us younger men from making mistakes that they had made. Dick Applin, who I called "Uncle Dick," told us at his 20th Company Anniversary party that he had not taken the time to take his daughter fishing. It took a lot of guts to get up and share that. I never forgot his words and respected him for saying it. Mr. Benza, the district manager, often had parties and outings for the salesmen. We worked tremendously hard under a lot of pressure and we played equally hard. Insurance agents love to party!

My sales were going well. It was amazing how I'd wake up on Monday morning not knowing where my next sale would come from, but by the week's end, I'd have sold several new policies. The public liked and trusted me. I felt most comfortable selling to young couples, like Sandy and myself, or men getting out of the service. One of my new clients was Steve Rex. Steve had just come home from the Coast Guard, married his childhood sweetheart, bought a mobile home, and celebrated the birth of his first child, a daughter. His life paralleled my own.

On the Fourth of July 1971, Steve was planting a new lawn when the tractor tipped over and killed him. I was totally shocked! My mind returned to Vietnam and all the carnage I had seen. I prepared to visit Steve's parents and widow. That familiar, guilty feeling reappeared. "Why did Steve have to die while I could continue to enjoy my life and watch my baby girl grow?" I wondered as my anguish continued. As difficult as this was, I felt good about having sold Steve the life insurance. I knew it would make a big difference in the future of his family. Convinced of the value of this business, I continued to sell with a vengeance and determination that I did not have prior to this first death claim. As an insurance agent, I had made a difference in the lives of Steve's widow and orphan.

Tim Conway had hired some new people so it gave me a break. I still saw him at the district office on Thursdays, which usually resulted in some kind of confrontation. One day, I was talking on the telephone when he kept interrupting me. I politely asked him to keep quiet, but he persisted telling me to hang up the phone, as he needed to speak with me that instant. When I didn't comply, he reached for the phone. As he did so, I turned to him and said, "Conway leave me alone or I'll shove this phone down your throat." The other men shuddered, then laughed. I was telling him exactly what they were thinking.

The year was going well for me except for having to deal with Tim. I used to imagine him in Vietnam as a grunt. "He wouldn't last a week," I thought. I definitely wouldn't want him sharing my foxhole or walking point for me. Subconsciously, I often used that analogy with people I'd meet. I judged them based on how I pictured them performing in a combat situation.

Late that summer, Conway called me on the spur of the moment.

"I'm coming over to work with you."

"Tim, I have a dentist appointment," hoping that would end his plans for the day.

"What time?"

"3:30."

"I'll be over by noon and we can get a few hours in."

I was determined I'd keep my cool with him. These explosive episodes were wearing on my nerves. So when he arrived, I was on my best behavior. We got in my car to make some calls on customers. This "visit" turned out to be an unannounced audit. Although this was a normal procedure, I had never been audited. I had the strong feeling that Conway was digging for some dishonest act on my part. I knew I had nothing to worry about. We stopped at several clients' homes where he checked the customers' records against mine. While driving he started discussing my lapse record. I had improved the condition of my debit considerably by going out of my way to service the clients and collecting their premiums. I told Tim that I was pretty pleased with my performance. He started comparing my record to Dick Applin's.

I kept my mouth shut as long as I could, but I couldn't any longer.

"Tim, why are you comparing me to Dick? I've been with the Company for a year and a half and Dick's been in the business for twenty years. I don't give a shit about his lapse record."

"Well, you should care," he began to shout.

"That's it. I'm taking you back to your car," I shouted as I did a U-turn in the middle of the highway. Conway was furious. I pulled into my driveway and told him I was leaving for the dentist. Before I could stop him, he grabbed my debit book and took off yelling, "You're done," as he drove away. Again, I thought I was fired. The next day, I drove to the district office to see what my status was. It no longer mattered to me; I'd had enough of this "Mickey Mouse" game.

Meanwhile, Jim McGlaughlin, my Veterans Counselor had suggested that I take the test for the New York State Veterans Counselor position. Although I lacked a college education, they accepted equivalent experience. Jim helped me create an impressive application that was accepted. I was allowed to sit for the exam. I received the results earlier in the week. My grade was 87, but I was given 10 additional preference points for being a disabled Veteran, which raised my grade to 97. I assumed I had an excellent chance of being appointed.

When I arrived at the office, I asked Conway for my debit book. He wouldn't give it back and walked away from me. I took my moneybag and threw it at him. "If you want the book, take the money too." The ball was in his court now. He suddenly reappeared and said smugly, "Mr. Benza wants to see you in his office now!" I must admit I felt like a kid being sent to the principal's office. Again, my mind flashed back to Nam, this was Article 15 time all over again. Conway began telling Mr. Benza about all my shortcomings as I listened patiently. When he finished, I looked at the District Manager.

"Would you mind if I spoke to you alone?"

Tim started to protest and dominated the conversation until I looked at Ray Benza.

"Mr. Benza, this is your office isn't it?"

Ray looked surprised. "Yes, it is," he said, and then he asked Tim to leave.

I proceeded to tell him how I enjoyed the job and was doing the best I could. "Conway doesn't know how to manage people," I told him. "It doesn't matter because I've had enough of this, I'm leaving." Ray Benza commented about Tim being young and I smiled saying, "Sir, he's three years older than I am." Then he dropped a bombshell, swearing me to secrecy. "I can't tell you everything, but please sit tight. I promise there is change coming and Conway won't be part of it." He closed by saying, "You're doing a fine job and here is your debit book and money bag."

As I exited the building, I wasn't sure if I'd stay. I would have to see how my upcoming interview went. A score of 97 would be hard to beat. Sandy and I drove to Rochester, N.Y. for my interview. When we got to the State Office Building, I was told that the position had been filled the day prior. "How could that be?" I asked. "I wasn't even interviewed." I later learned that the new Veterans Counselor for the State was a recently retired Army Colonel who had only scored 85 on the exam. Who said life was fair? At work, Conway stayed away from me.

In the meantime, Sandy and I enjoyed making new friends in Cohocton and raising our daughter. We spent a lot of our free time with my folks. Sandy and Mom went grocery shopping together each Thursday. We'd spend Sundays with them, enjoying Mom's ethnic cooking. Dad and I enjoyed discussing politics, current events, and finance. Debbie enjoyed "Granny" and "Pa", too. It was in the fall of that year that Mr. Benza's secret was announced. The Hornell District Office was being closed. Half of the agents would work out of the Batavia, N.Y. district; the others would join the Corning, N.Y. district. Mr. Benza would hand pick his sales team and we would work out of a detached office in Dansville, N.Y. Andy Murphy would get the other men and they would remain in an office in Hornell. Tim Conway was being sent to Corning. Eventually his management career came to an end. He became an agent again and soon after he left the insurance business. Along the way, he lost his wife and children to a nasty divorce.

Chapter 33

FAMILY AND BUSINESS GROWTH

It was now 1972 and Mr. Russell Rose was our Batavia, N.Y. district manager. Batavia was one of Metropolitan's best district offices in New York State. Mr. Rose had a reputation as a tough manager, but one who cared as much about his employees as he did striving to be number one. Although Ray Benza's job as manager of a detached office was somewhat of a step backward, he actually made more money than he did in his previous position. He was now back in the "trenches" so to speak and would be required to go on sales calls with his agents, something he hadn't done in a number of years. It was a difficult transition, but he handled it well.

The older agents didn't enjoy having a manager shadowing them. It didn't bother me; I liked Ray and he got excited when we worked together. I would give 150% in an effort to impress him with my selling talent. Sandy always invited Ray to have supper with us even though he offered to go to the local diner. We enjoyed his company. We would all attend sales meetings on Fridays at the Masonic Temple in Dansville and later in a room over the newspaper office. Our unit enjoyed the affiliation with the Batavia district.

In the spring of that year, Ray decided to have an outing at the Sportsman's Club in Hornell. All the original employees of the now defunct Hornell district would be invited. Ray worked for days preparing the main meal, which was to be an Italian feast. The men enjoyed the opportunity to relax and enjoy an afternoon of talking, playing cards, and sharing ideas over a beer or two. I saw Ray walking through the dining area with a handful of firewood for the fireplace. He suddenly dropped to one knee with a pained look on his face. Several guys laughed thinking Ray was pulling a stunt. Soon it was obvious that he was in trouble and we rushed to his side while at the same time calling an ambulance. Andy Murphy rode to the hospital with the ambulance. We all waited nervously and the mood of our party changed significantly. When Andy returned, he told us Ray was dead. I remember driving to my Mom's house and breaking down in tears.

Death again touched my life. I had lost so many people in my short life, my Father, Wink Wolfgruber, Mr. Timmerman, many close friends in the War, and now Ray. I would never forget the encouragement Ray gave me. He once told someone that, "I was the best thing to come down the pipe in a long time." During my conflict with Conway, I would probably have quit had it not been for Ray. Subconsciously thoughts of Vietnam began to enter my mind along with thoughts of all the death I had seen. We salesmen served as the pallbearers at Ray's funeral, and by Monday morning, we were all back to work.

Russ Rose drove to Dansville each Friday to conduct our sales meetings and to meet with us individually. I liked him from the start and had a lot of respect for him. He had lost a leg in a bread truck accident many years before, but he did not let that keep him from carving out a successful insurance career. Russ saw something in me, potential I suspect. To this day Russ tells me that I was somewhat of a "wise ass," a real "ball buster," a "diamond in the rough." He did see potential and knew how to motivate and manage me. Somewhere along the line, he convinced me to challenge the more experienced men. He convinced me that I could accomplish whatever I wanted in life. Through my association with Russ and the other professionals in the Batavia district office, I raised my sights not only in my production goals, but also in my personal goals. I felt my dreams could become reality if I worked hard and learned the traits of successful people.

I knew what it was like to be broke, I knew what hard work was, and I had suffered physical and mental discomfort. I did not know what it felt like to have cash in my pocket. My perception of wealth was to have both a fireplace and wall-to-wall carpeting in the house. If I worked hard for the next twenty-five years, perhaps by the time I was fifty, life would be easy for me. I deserved this, as did Sandy and our child. It was a conscious decision on our part. I would sacrifice time at home in order to provide for my family's future. I wanted them to have opportunities that I never had. There was a more private reason too. I owed this to my Father and to the men who died in Vietnam.

It was at a district outing that Russ made the comment that if I sold enough insurance to qualify for the Company's "Honor Club" I would be offered Ray Benza's job. He had been drinking heavily that day, but we all heard him. Since Mr. Benza's death we were all wondering who would replace Ray. Most of the older men on our staff weren't interested in management. Some of them had tried management when they were younger and were not successful.

It was a high-pressure job since you received pressure from the salesmen as well as the company. Not only was the manager responsible for production, but he also had to recruit new salesmen, train them and see that each man met his quotas. Additionally, managers were expected to enroll in advanced education courses, as well as learn about new products introduced by the company so they could teach them to their staff. It was a young man's job and a tough one.

The rest of that year was a challenge because all of us were having a good sales year. Russ Rose seemed to always be pitting me up against Dick Applin. He probably felt a friendly race would benefit us both. Dick and I were neck and neck right to the end of the year. I believe there may have been a couple salesmen with better production than both of us. As the final figures were recorded each week, Dick and I would exchange positions. One week he was ahead of me, the next week I'd move ahead of him. It came down to the final week. I really pushed myself working Saturday of that week. Russ was calling for any last minute sales, and at the same time would give us the up-to-date figures. I had enough sales to beat Dick, but I decided not to report them. I decided to let Dick win. He had been placed in a difficult situation with this challenge. He would lose face being beaten by a rookie. I'd received plenty of praise and recognition; it served no useful purpose to defeat Dick. Our office had a great year! There was still no word on who the new manager would be.

Russ never again brought up the subject of me getting Ray's job. Perhaps he had forgotten his comment and challenge to me earlier that year. It didn't matter, I wasn't certain I wanted to be manager. I was doing fine as a salesman with no one to worry about but myself. It was ironic that this was my same attitude in the Army. I was offered Officers Candidate School, but beyond spending the extra year in the service, I had not wanted to be responsible for others. It was easier to just take care of "number one."

Life was changing whether I welcomed it or not. I was being put into positions of responsibility. My biggest fear was that we would get a new manager like Tim Conway, and the others certainly felt the same.

The holidays were approaching and another year had passed. The third anniversary of Mole City was approaching as well. Sure, I thought about Vietnam, but I did my best to bury it. Several of my customers had sons in Vietnam and would mention it to me. It was obvious from the way some of them looked at me that they wondered why someone my age wasn't in the service. They were surprised when I told them I'd been in Vietnam myself. I seldom shared the details of my service with them.

As the new year began and winter turned to the spring of 1972, I continued to do well at Met Life. Sandy surprised me with the news that we were pregnant again. We hadn't planned on that, but we were happy. Our mobile home and car were too small for a family of four. It was about this time that Russ called me and invited me to Batavia to join him for lunch. He offered me the job as manager of the Dansville Office. I was just shy of my twenty-fifth birthday. Sandy and I discussed the opportunity. As usual, she was supportive of any decision I made. My Father and I discussed the decision, but I wasn't sure I could handle the responsibility. Dad said, "They wouldn't offer you the job if they didn't think you could do it." Weighing all the pros and cons and considering I could end up working for another Conway, I decided to accept the promotion. It would not be easy managing older, more experienced agents, particularly the same people I'd worked with the past couple of years. I knew I could do this if I put my mind to it, after all if I could survive Vietnam, I could survive anything life threw at me.

Chapter 34

BUSINESS SUCCESS

There was no "honeymoon" period. Russ threw me into the fire immediately. Manpower was a priority so I began recruiting. My first hiree was Eddie Schneider, a local Cohocton boy who was recently married. He and I got off to a great start attaining his sales quotas. Within three weeks, I hired another young man, Eddie Henderson. Both of these men were hard workers and self motivated. Russ was elated. It seemed like whatever he asked me to do got done. My income skyrocketed! As a twenty-five-year old, non-college graduate, three years out of the Army, I was earning over $25,000 a year! The average income at that time was $9-10,000. I was gone most of the time, but I justified my absence by what I could do for my family with my earnings. Sandy and I did agree that I should be home for dinner with the family. So for the next ten years, I made it a priority to be home by 4:30, so we could eat at 5:00, and most of the time I'd return to work by 6:00. I would usually return home by 10:30 or 11:00, wound up like a kite. I'd have two Manhattan cocktails while I watched Johnny Carson and then I'd go to bed. In the morning, I would be out of the house by 7:30 or 8:00. It was a fast paced, high-pressure job that kept me so busy I had no time to think about my past life as a soldier.

The only two connections to that time period were when the POWs were brought home. I cancelled all my appointments and came home in the middle of the day to watch them arriving at Clark Air Force Base. The other time was when the parents of David Briggs visited me. They apparently waited around all day for me to get home for dinner. They brought Debbie a doll. Mr. and Mrs. Briggs did not accept or believe that Dave was dead. They asked if I knew Dave; I told them I did. They showed me a picture of Dave and said, "Is this the same Dave you knew?" Again I said, "Yes, it is." Then Mrs. Briggs asked, "Did you see his body?" "No, I did not. I could have, but chose not to." Apparently his casket had been closed and they never were able to view his remains. Without giving them details of their son's death, I assured them he had died quickly. I went on to tell them how well liked Dave was by his peers and what a good soldier he was. They departed no better off than they were and I believed they were glad. They did not want to close this chapter of their lives as painful as it was. Since I did not see his body, they continued to hope that he was still alive.

I enjoyed my new position. I approached each new challenge as a "mission." Sandy and I attended our first Honor Club that year in Illinois. It was the first of many. We were able to go to the Playboy Club in the Poconos, Hilton Head Island, Host Farms, Pinehurst, North Carolina and several other famous resorts.

In December of 1972, our son Johnny was born. I traded the Mustang for a new Thunderbird and sold the mobile home in order to buy a house. We found a modest ranch style home in Cohocton and immediately added a large addition with wall-to-wall carpeting and a fireplace that covered an entire wall! Not everyone appreciated our good fortune. My sister heard the news and quickly began plans to build a house too. Some of the locals couldn't understand how someone who came to town with nothing and lived in a trailer could move up the economic scale so quickly. Others criticized me for working too much. That was the trouble with small towns: the pettiness and envy within them.

Cohocton was even more that way because it was somewhat isolated. People could be envious and try to out do each other. Sandy and I did not like this and got tired of defending our lifestyle. Our motives were not understood. It was not about money, or keeping up with the Jones', or trying to impress others. We were motivated by our parents who worked long and hard, and did their best to provide for the family. I was also a first-generation American with immigrant values.

My sales team had a great year and I asked Russ for a real office. My men deserved more than meeting over a print shop and I needed a secretary. If we were professionals, then let us project that image. I found an excellent building in a good location. We had it re-carpeted and we obtained a desk for each man. I had a private office and there was a reception area for our new secretary. My salesmen were very supportive of me.

There were times that were difficult for me as a manager. When a man's production was down, I took the "heat" for it and in turn had to confront the salesman about it. Sometimes these confrontations were resented. I did my absolute best to keep the pressure off my men, but I did have objectives to achieve and I would reach my goals either with them or with new hires. Whenever I worked with a member of my staff, I gave 110% to make our assignment successful and to put money in their pockets. From a somewhat egotistical standpoint, I would ask them to line up sales calls with prospects they were not able to close. If I made the sale for them, which I often did, then I had earned their respect. I never asked anyone to do anything that I myself wouldn't do.

Russ had instilled in me the need to take care of my men and their families. This was easy for me because I grew to love each one of them. I got involved in their personal lives and problems. When they were troubled, so was I. During my tenure as manager, I never drank while working. I assured every wife that if her husband were with me that he would be working and not drinking. Some managers had a reputation for working at night, making some sales and then hitting a local bar or Legion Post with their salesman in tow. The wives would be upset and rightfully so. Unfortunately, every so often on Friday afternoons when work was over, I drank. Sometimes I would come home loaded. My excuse was I worked hard all week and needed to get some relief from the stress.

My reputation as a manager grew. I normally finished in the top 5 or 10 sales managers. Once, I was number 3 out of 100 managers in New York State. When Metropolitan entered the Property and Casualty business in 1978, my sales team led all the offices from Albany to Buffalo. I was the number one manager in 1978 and 1979. When I was twenty-eight-years old, I was diagnosed with hypertension. It was discovered while taking a paramedic exam for the purchase of life insurance. I was furious that my own employer wanted to charge me extra for my life insurance, implying that I was a risk. If I was such a risk, then why was I able to work sixty hours a week? Perhaps I should be on disability! When I contacted Dr. Wolfgurber, he read me the "riot act." "Insurance companies publish so many booklets on health and welfare, yet most insurance executives abuse themselves horribly. Many suffer heart attacks at a young age." He then scolded me for not taking the time to come to him for my medical exam instead of seeing a paramedic in my office. He eventually prescribed medication for my high blood pressure.

During this time frame, my brother Joe became eligible for the draft. I told my folks to get him in the reserves, which they did. He liked it and has spent over thirty years in the active reserves. I could not have lived with myself if I'd allowed him to endure the same fate I had.

Mom and Dad were aging as their children all grew into adults. Joe and Bob both graduated from college at Alfred. Joe stayed home to work on the farm. Bob took off after college and was never around much after that. My family continued to spend weekends with my folks. Dad sold us a piece of scrubland where I had a pond built. We bought a 1926 N.Y. Central Railroad caboose and I converted it into a vacation home. Debbie and Johnny learned to swim at our camp and we'd enjoy our weekends up there. Dad loved the place and would visit us on weekends.

We spent many of our holidays in Arkport and many of them were ruined due to confrontations with Jean. She was jealous of me and I never knew why. After all, she had a nice home and Mike had a good job as an engineer at Eastman Kodak. It was not like anyone had given me anything. She would belittle me any time she could. She began to tell my children how stupid I was in school, that I was lousy in math, and that I flunked out of college. I could put up with her attacks on me, but when she picked on Sandy or my children, I'd fly into a rage. This would then cause her to lose it completely. One Thanksgiving with Sandy, Johnny and Debbie present, she said, "I wish you had died in Vietnam." I never realized how painful her words were until they surfaced some twenty years later during a therapy session.

I didn't want my family near her and sometimes we would go many months, even years, with no contact. My Mother was always the peacemaker. She would say, "Yanko, make up with her, forget it, make peace for me." She would tell me that she loved Jean because she was her daughter even though she did not like her much.

During these years of raising my family, becoming successful in my career, and respected in the community, my Father became extremely proud of me. He would often refer to me as "my son" when talking to people. I think he had been somewhat disappointed that his sons had not gone into farming, but now he knew that I had made the right choice. He confided to me that I was earning more than the potato farmers in the county.

Chapter 35

SANDY JOINS MY CHURCH

As I grew older, the pressures intensified. The insurance industry was changing. I acknowledged that I was a workaholic. The only way I could get away from work was to literally leave the State. Sandy and I would take the children and vacation in Virginia Beach, Canada, or Florida. During those early years, I was involved in the community. I was President of the Lions Club and enjoyed delivering Christmas Baskets to the needy. We participated in the activities of St. Pius Church and tried to attend Mass each Sunday. Eventually, we sent our children to the Catholic school in Wayland.

One day when I came home at lunchtime Fr. Erb, the local Priest, was there. Unbeknownst to me, Sandy had decided to convert to Catholicism. I was surprised, to say the least. She had weekly lessons with the priest. She explained that she always went to church with Debbie, Johnny and me, but felt like an outsider. She really liked Fr. Erb so she decided to convert with his assistance. The priest was surprised when I told him that we hadn't been married in the Catholic Church. The Catholic Church did not validate our marriage for that reason. Sandy wanted to invite our parents to the service where she would receive communion and be confirmed. My Mom and Dad were surprised, but happy. I'm certain it had been difficult to see their son married outside our Church since they were both practicing Catholics and products of generations of Catholics before them.

Following Sandy's ceremony, I was called forward and the priest very discreetly performed a Catholic marriage ceremony that validated our marriage in the "eyes" of the Catholic Church. Afterward, we had a celebration dinner at our house. Sandy's parents were very "cool" and visibly upset all evening. Before the evening ended her mother created a scene. She was terribly upset by the events of the evening. I sensed that she also realized how close Sandy and my Mom had become. It was embarrassing for us to see her parent's outburst in front of the priest. Her folks departed hastily shouting, "She's still our daughter." This episode put a damper on my relationship with my in-laws for many years. Siding with me over her parents put Sandy in a terrible place. It was unfortunate as it was a loss for all of us. That's the sad thing about the past — you can't change it. Fortunately time has a healing effect and today I am close to both of Sandy's parents.

My career continued to grow. I had my ups and downs. I hired new men and lost them. Some were not cut out for the business or had wives that were not supportive. I would no longer hire anyone unless they were high quality individuals with proven success patterns and wives that would support them with their efforts to succeed. I was thirty-two years old now and we drove a new Cadillac. My employer felt it important that its managers project a specific corporate image. Since 50% of my job was to recruit new agents, it was important to convey success. We also lived in a lovely home and owned a vacation house. I was living proof that a man or woman could make money in the insurance business. I still worked sixty-hour weeks. I'd see the children for a few minutes in the morning and again at the supper table, but they'd be in bed by the time I got home at night. I did try to spend all weekend with them. They were growing up quickly.

Chapter 36

A PRICE FOR SUCCESS

I recruited some high quality salespeople and trained them thoroughly so that they too became successful. I owed them that and took my responsibility seriously. The problem was that after four or five years they would seek less stressful jobs within the industry. It became somewhat of a joke, "Get a job with Metropolitan, let Senka train you and then find a better position somewhere else." Other insurance businesses would laugh that Senka was their trainer. They knew if I had trained a man or woman that he or she would probably make a high quality employee. The majority of the people I recruited still work in the insurance industry and most are still my friends. It became extremely difficult and frustrating for me to recruit, train, and then lose an employee. I wondered how long I could keep up this maddening pace.

My top producers were still my older salesmen, Appy, Stosh Sager, Bob Powell, Bob Wood, Clete Fries and Bobby Wiseman. They were all in their fifties and would be retiring in the next ten years. I admired them for the job they were doing. They worked long hours, a lot of night calls and saw many changes. It had to be difficult, but they met the challenge. I now understand why Tom Brokaw called these World War II Vets the "Greatest Generation."

Unless I was promoted to a district sales manager, my career would become continually more difficult. In 1980, nine years from the time Johnny was born, Sandy announced that we were pregnant again. She had not really wanted more children, but I had a sincere desire to have another baby knowing that in ten years Debbie and Johnny would be in college and Sandy and I would only be in our forty's and still working. Most people assume that when a couple has such a gap between children that the baby was a late life accident. It was just the opposite with us. Our third son Jeff was the only one of our children that we planned. Jeffery was born July 2, 1981. We hadn't seen my sister for over a year but asked her adult children to be Jeff's Godparents. Eventually at the urging of my Mother, we allowed Jean to attend the baptism and she was back in our lives again.

Debbie would be going to high school in a couple of years and the pressures of work became more intense. My income was not keeping pace with times and I now had to sell a policy from time to time to add to my income. I never competed with my men and limited my sales to about five per year.

In 1982, I began to lose much of my enthusiasm for work. Money to a large extent was not as important as time. I realized time was my scarcest commodity. I actually envied people who had adequate time to enjoy their lives. This actually caused problems and may have even cost us close friendships. Ted and his wife, Lorraine, were very close to Sandy and me. Jim, a friend from the '60s, had moved into the area with his family. They became friends with Ted and Lorraine through us, and that was fine. As much as I liked both couples, there would be times I'd want to talk to Ted and we would plan our schedules ahead of time so we could take an evening off from work. I'd get to Ted's house and within ten minutes Jim and his wife would drop in unexpectedly. So we sacrificed a night off for nothing. People who worked 9 to 5 had no idea how valuable time was for people like us. I'm sure both couples felt that I was acting "funny" and it eventually caused the friendships to deteriorate. Even today, I feel this was a loss because Sandy and I liked both couples very much.

Chapter 37

FATHER'S DEATH UNEXPECTED

1983 was a tough year from the onset. Eddie Schneider was promoted to Sales Manager in Hornell. He had worked hard and deserved the promotion. Jim Shanley resigned to sell Savings Bank life insurance and Tom Didas went to work for the Reidman Corporation. I lost three men and then one of the older men announced his retirement. What else could go wrong? In early March, I called my Mom since we hadn't been able to visit that weekend. She was crying and said my Father was in bed with the flu and chest pains. I told her he should be in the hospital. "He won't go," she replied. "Tell Dad I'm on my way and I'm taking him to the hospital." When I reached her home, I discovered Dad had driven himself to the hospital and they admitted him. He had suffered a heart attack three days earlier!

Sandy and I drove to see him. He looked very frightened but otherwise he seemed fine. He complained about gas pains. Dad talked about ordering his seed potato for the spring planting and was concerned that he still had a full warehouse to ship. We visited awhile and I shook his hand, said goodbye and went back to my Mom's for the afternoon. We had dinner and drove back to see my Dad. When we got there his bed was empty. "What the hell is going on," I wondered. Then I saw them push my Dad past us on a gurney, his eyes were closed. "Oh no!" I thought. Soon Doc Wolfgruber solemnly walked towards us shaking his head. "I'm sorry. We tried to install a pacemaker." "Is he dead?" He nodded his head as we all broke down sobbing. This is a nightmare! Is this really happening? I could see that I had to put on a strong front for everyone's sake. Dad was everyone's pillar of strength, we all depended on him, went to him with our problems, but now he was gone at the age of seventy-one. Everyone turned to me. It was the European custom for the oldest son to assume the position as head of the family. I knew Mom desperately needed someone to lean on — she was scared to death. I assured her everything would be fine and I promised her I would not let anything happen to her. The only time I allowed myself to cry was when I was in the shower. Like in Vietnam, I didn't have time to grieve.

I called Russ Rose. "Russ not only have I lost four salesmen, but I've lost my Father, too." Russ was sympathetic and told me to take all the time I needed. Being a businessman, I began to put together a plan in my head. There was so much to do. This was about more than losing my Dad; there was a warehouse full of perishable goods, a spring planting ahead, and the lifetime of a man's work. We called Bob in Wyoming to break the news and then Joe and I went to the funeral home to make arrangements. I was surprised to learn that Mom knew absolutely nothing about my Dad's finances. Apparently he preferred it that way. It was a volatile "cutthroat" business and I suspect he preferred to carry the burden alone and not cause my Mom additional worry.

It was a beautiful funeral if the formality of saying goodbye to a loved one for the last time can be described as beautiful. Bob and I both gave moving eulogies for our Father. Neighboring potato farmers served as pallbearers.

Chapter 38

FACING BUSINESS CHALLENGES

As soon as my Father was buried, I began to deal with his business. I found the contracts for his crop in the warehouse. Why the hell hadn't he been shipping? It was expensive paying $800 – 900 per month in heating bills. I contacted Wise and Frito Lay and they authorized me to ship. We couldn't have done this without the help of Tom Hoeffner, Charlie and Henry Wolfurst and the Horan brothers. They were experienced farmers and lifelong friends of my Father. Whenever I handed them a check for their work, they would tear them up in front of me. I was touched by their friendship and generosity and have never forgotten what they did for our family.

Our first two loads were rejected. They said that they did not meet chipping standards. I knew it was a lie and Tom Hoeffner confirmed it. Apparently, the potato chip companies had an abundance of potatoes and would do whatever they could to "weasel" out of their contracts. Considering that they would no longer be doing business with Joe Katsur Sr., it was just an added incentive to renege on the contract. I found Wise in particular to be cold and heartless in the way they treated a hard working farmer's family after a lifelong business relationship. Since that time, I've asked Sandy not to buy their food products.

My Dad, Joe Katsur had been a prosperous potato grower since 1939. He was the second person to move to Steuben County from Hicksville Long Island but the first to have a successful commercial potato growing operation. At the time of his death, he had grown potatoes longer than any other farmer in Steuben County.

We were paid nothing for three tractor-trailers full of spuds. After that I turned off the heat in the warehouse and decided to empty the warehouse, bag by bag, shovel by shovel. We sold them for $1 per 100-pound bag. Even at that, people complained. One guy even ran off with twenty bags without paying us. It did keep my Mom, Joe, and his wife busy. This gave me time to plan my own strategy for the family. Some days I would report to my office dressed in a three-piece suit and by noon I was in the dirty warehouse shoveling potatoes in my business attire. Sandy and my children even worked.

When I met with the banks and creditors, I walked away shocked. Dad had spent a quarter of a million dollars to plant his crop. Not being paid by the potato chip companies after his sudden death left his estate in serious financial difficulty. My Mom could lose everything including the home she loved. I sat down with Joe and Mom and broke the bad news to them. I asked Joe if he wanted to assume these debts in exchange for the farmland and all the equipment. I pointed out that if he could not run a successful farm operation he could lose the land. His other option was to find a job and let me deal with the mess. I assured him that I would help him find employment. He decided not to take responsibility for the farm and within a few weeks, he was working. As for my Mom, I told her that she was officially retired. She had worked hard her entire life and she deserved to enjoy her remaining years.

Trying to settle my Dad's affairs was stressful and time consuming. At one point, it caused friction between Russ and me. He felt it was time for me to get back to giving 110% to Metropolitan. He said my responsibility was to Sandy and the children. "Wrong," I said. "I'm responsible for everyone, especially my Mother who did so much for me." I decided if this conflict cost me my job then, I would pay that price. This entire episode had now changed my priorities. I had to take a good hard look at who I was and where I was going. I knew there needed to be changes in my own life, but first I had to solve this problem. I knew this would be a challenge, a challenge that had to be met. A man's life work was at stake. My Mother's future was in my hands. I knew I would eventually resolve this as I had all the many challenges I had faced during my life.

Since Vietnam, I was confident I could handle anything that was thrown at me. I had proven that during the fourteen years at Met Life. All my "missions" were accomplished year after year. I was the guy that always came through in a "pinch," when the "chips were down." When my friends and associates had problems, they would seek my advice. I was no longer afraid of responsibility; it was a part of life. Solving problems was satisfying and rewarding. I genuinely enjoyed helping others.

I felt I could not concentrate on my own future. I had recently been appointed to Metropolitan's Company Advisory Council. This was a highly prestigious position. I had the opportunity of putting real input into decisions that would affect salespeople and sales managers. On several occasions, I met with Company level officers in the Home Office. I knew several vice presidents on a first name basis. None of this seemed important to me anymore. I began to inquire about other opportunities. I even considered returning to personal sales. I was positive that at the age of thirty-five, I was "burnt out."

Chapter 39

CHANGING COURSE

Eventually, I met a man named Paul Branch. Paul had developed a new concept of marketing insurance in rural America and was looking for partners. I spoke to some of the partners and I decided this was not only a sound business opportunity, but also a change I needed. It would necessitate moving away, but would enable me to own my own agency and be able to spend more time with my family. Money was no longer the issue. I wanted to be able to watch the children play ball, go to their concerts, and be there for them. I wasn't drinking much anymore. One time, Debbie and Johnny found me sick on the bathroom floor and asked Sandy what was wrong with dad. After that, I promised myself they would never again see me like that. I had several job offers closer to home, but Sandy and I felt we all needed this change. It was 1982. Debbie was in the 7th grade, Johnny in the 4th, and Jeff was one-year old.

We would be moving to Schuyler County near Elmira and Ithaca, N.Y. The children would have many more opportunities available to them. Telling Russ Rose and my salesmen that I was leaving was extremely difficult. The feeling was similar to how I felt returning home when my buddies were still fighting in

Charlie Company. I would miss these fellows who had all become like fathers to me. I learned much later that Russ was not happy when I resigned. The day following my resignation, Greg Doby, the regional manager, requested I come to Buffalo to meet with him. My last conversation with Doby pertained to a District Manager's position in Corning, N.Y. He wouldn't promote me because Corning was no longer in his region; thus he would lose me. I thought that was pretty selfish of him and told him so. After all, I had worked like a horse for fourteen years for the Company. Politics should not have held me back.

When I arrived in Buffalo, Doby asked my reasons for leaving. I stated I needed more time with my family and less stress. When he quickly offered me a Field Training Consultant's position, I laughed. "Didn't you hear me, Greg," I asked. "Why would I take a position where there is greater stress and I would have to live out of a suitcase?" I asked him about a district manager's job in Franklinville, N.Y. I had been friends with Frank Valvo, the previous manager, who had suffered a severe stroke. Greg said that he would "consider" me for the job. I laughed and told him goodbye! My job at Met Life was a real security blanket for me. Resigning was a risk that I hoped would prove to be to everyone's benefit. I was scared. "At least they won't be shooting at me," I thought.

With Joe working and the warehouse cleaned out, I now had time to put my plan in writing. The equipment could be sold, some odd parcels of land as well, there were debts owed to Dad that I had to collect, and some seed to be sold. My plan was to pay the debt in five years, but it was rejected. I did not give up, but rather prepared another. This time it would necessitate selling the farmland. It was my hope that each of my siblings as well as myself would be willing to buy a part of the farm. In this way, the land would remain in the family and the monies would go towards the estate debt. I also asked Joe to look into government lease programs.

According to my Mother, Jean told her that she and Mike wanted no part of the farm. I still wrote to everyone regarding my plan. Joe, Bob, and I agreed to buy half the farm, and the other half would be sold to an outsider. A close friend of Dad's wanted the farm as he had hunted there for forty years. I submitted the plan and told the banks that this was my final offer. They could accept it or devise their own plan. They accepted my plan and I put things in motion. The land sales were made and my brother Bob agreed to come home to fix and paint the machinery. I then accumulated and invested enough funds to assure my Mother an adequate cash flow for her living expenses.

We moved to Montour Falls, N.Y. and bought a new home. It was much larger than the old one. We had five bedrooms and three full bathrooms with a four-acre lot, which included a forest and trout stream. I hadn't sold the Cohocton house so I was paying on two mortgages. We liked the beauty of the area, the gorges, the grape vineyards, the waterfalls, and the great Seneca Lake. The Fingerlakes were indeed gorgeous. This was a tourist area with a racetrack nearby. The children would go to public school rather than the Catholic School, which disappointed us, but elated Johnny.

The agency we purchased had been in Odessa, N.Y. since 1929 through various ownerships. The current owner was a man named Bob. Bob was ill at the age of fifty-six and had decided to sell his agency. The agreement was that he would stay with me for one year and then retire. I liked him. He was very quiet and laid back, not at all like me. It was a characteristic that I hoped would rub off. I needed to find some peace and serenity in my life.

Chapter 40

BONDINGS

As soon as we moved to Odessa, a million things went wrong. Everything from the furnace blowing up to the water pump quitting. We wondered if this was a bad omen telling us we'd made a mistake. The two older children made friends quickly at school and in the neighborhood. Jeff, who was a year old, was still upset about leaving his home. As young as he was, he knew his life had changed. I had a tremendous adjustment to make. I felt like the "odd duck." I didn't know the area or the clients, and lacked expertise in property and casualty insurance. I had no experience with commercial insurance. The three office employees, Jan, Ruth, and Carol, were helpful. Bob offered some help, but was not a student of the business. Rather than giving me a wrong answer, he would say research that yourself.

When 5 o'clock came, I couldn't accept that the workday was over. It didn't seem right because I had always worked until late at night. Sandy and Bob said that I was like a caged animal. I would walk around the house wearing my business suit. It actually took me almost a year to calm down. I enjoyed this business much better than Met Life.

Sandy and I made many friends, primarily through Debbie, Johnny, and Jeff. I started over again getting involved in the community. I had time to go to little league games, swim meets, and scout meetings. Several of my associates at Metropolitan asked me to help them make a career change. They were all hard workers and were burning themselves out. I sympathized with them. I helped John Chrisman, Dave and George Spinnegan, and Dan Wensel obtain insurance agencies through our Iroquois Group.

My management style was different. I was very open with the office staff. My philosophy was that we should enjoy coming to work and that we were adults who had a job to do. I allowed them to have a radio and Sandy and I would join them for Christmas parties and other special occasions. I did not accept underwriting or claims decisions as final. I would "fight" to assist a client in getting a claim paid or a policy issued. I had a lot to learn, and during that first year I was under a great deal of stress. We had an obligation to pay the former owner a considerable amount of money over the next ten years. I had a family to support and I had to free my Mother of her financial dilemma. I had no choice but to make this work. Gradually, everything started falling into place.

Bob retired and Sandy and I organized a lovely party for him. We invited his family, friends, and business associates. We had an auction of Dad's equipment and then I sold my Cohocton home. I was on my own now, although Bob helped me anyway he could and I appreciated it. He had become a father figure to me, a replacement for my Dad and Russ Rose. I knew his retirement was my responsibility and I made certain he received his check on the first of each month. Within the first year, I had gained good insight into the business and the community.

It was during the early 1980's that I became reacquainted with some of my childhood friends with whom I'd lost contact. Charlie Schwarz moved from the Silicone Valley in San Jose, California to the suburbs of Boston. He, like myself, had little college, but became successful in the computer industry. We were older now and were not trying to compete with one another like when we were younger. We were genuinely interested in each other and enjoyed reminiscing about our childhood and teen years. Sandy and I were also reunited with Bev and John Hubric who now lived in Clearwater, Florida. John had become a plant manager for a computer chip company, but he too tired of the pressures and made a career change. He and Bev owned two successful Mobil convenience stores.

The late 1980's and '90's were busy, yet very happy for our family. Sandy and I enjoyed raising Debbie, Johnny and Jeff. We got involved with Odessa Montour Central School's sports boosters. Most of our friends had children who played sports with our kids. All three children were excellent swimmers. Johnny was a starter on the football team and track team. Deb was an excellent student and gave us few problems. Johnny on the other hand loved life and wherever there was trouble, he would find it. He disliked academics and we had to watch him carefully in order to keep him on the "right" path. Jeff was not a great student either, but he was not a discipline problem. He was a lovable, considerate boy. He was not the rough, tough type of kid like his older brother. We afforded our children every opportunity we could.

Johnny, Jeff, and Debbie

In the 1980s, we had foreign exchange students live with us. All three of our children traveled to Europe at least twice. Johnny, Deb and Jeff had their own personalities and the usual childhood squabbles yet they shared a genuine love for one another. Our children were our greatest source of pride. I had long ago promised myself that my children would not have a relationship such as the one I had with my sister. Whenever there was a disagreement, I would call a family meeting and we'd all say what was on our minds. Sometimes we would yell, scream, or cry, but when it was over, we were all friends again. We included my Mother in our family activities as much as possible.

Unfortunately, Jean would become so miserable at times that my Mom would give in to her demands rather than deal with the friction. It was for this reason that she was unable to spend as many holidays with us as she would have liked. Our family became very close to the Schwarz and Hubric families. John Hubric had been stricken with cancer; we often shared vacations and holidays together. We also continued to pay down the farm debt. My business was doing well even though the competition was keen. Our business increased each year. Debbie started college in 1988 and Johnny in 1992 after he spent some time in Madrid, Spain.

Jeff, Debbie, John, and Johnny

It was at this time that I surprised my Mother one afternoon with a handful of loans all marked "Paid In Full." She hugged me with tears in her eyes and said, "Yanko, I knew God saved you for a reason. When your Father died and following your birth, people said that this baby boy would someday take care of me and, sure enough, it is true." I believe that was one of the happiest days of my life. Because I made a difference, I solved a serious problem for my Mom. In a small way, I helped repay her for all she had done for me.

In 1992 Debbie graduated from college. She was the first one in our family with a four-year degree. We were so proud of her! Mom announced she was not coming to the graduation. We were heartbroken and could not understand why. Even today my eyes tear when I discuss this. We all attended graduation along with Sandy's folks. I learned several years later that my sister convinced Mom that people don't attend college graduations. My Mother always regretted not having attended. Neither of my sister's children ever finished college and apparently she just couldn't deal with the thought of her brother's children being college graduates.

Mom and I became very close after my Dad's death. We had always shared a special bond, but she seemed to feel secure knowing she had me to lean on. She often would divulge to me how smart she thought I was. She had watched me fight my share of battles in life and come out scarred but still standing. During Easter of 1993, I took my Mom to Florida with Sandy, Jeff and me. While the three of us went to Disney World, Mom stayed with Aunt Rose and Uncle Steve. Mom enjoyed talking and spending time with Rose. While we were there she had the opportunity to see Steve and Rose Hluchan as well. They were the couple that first introduced my Mother to my Father. Mom thoroughly enjoyed the visit to Florida.

When we were leaving Aunt Rose's house, my Mom said, "Yanko, Rose has no one to help them. If they ever need your help, don't be afraid to offer a helping hand." I assured her I would. She also remarked on the flight back how much she had enjoyed seeing the Hluchans. She then made a comment that I thought was odd at the time. She said something about not knowing how much longer she'd be around. I said, "Mom, you're seventy-five years old and walk faster than I do and offer to carry my bags in the airport. Your sisters are in their eighties and your mother was almost ninety when she died. So you'll be around a long time." She replied with a smile, "I don't think so." The flight was a disaster because we hit bad weather on a small shuttle plane and bounced all over the sky. I could see my Mom was scared so I held her hand and laughed, telling her everything was fine. Silently, I recited Hail Marys.

When we got back to our home, Mom spent the night. Again, she made some comment about not wanting to be in my shoes trying to settle her estate after she was gone. She joked that I'd need the State Police there. She anticipated big problems with my sister. She went home the next day and gave me a penholder made with laminated butterflies. This was her thanks for taking her to Florida.

Chapter 41

MY MOTHER'S PASSING

Two weeks later I returned to my office from a day in the field when my secretary gave me a message that changed my life. My Mother had been in an automobile accident. A State Trooper said that she was alive and at St. James Hospital in Hornell, N.Y. I immediately took off in my car, stopping only to get Sandy. When we arrived at the hospital, my Mom was in pain from a broken pelvis but would otherwise be okay. I looked at her car, which was a total wreck. It was a miracle that she had survived. I knew this was not the place for my Mom. After losing my Dad I had sworn that if anything ever happened to my Mom I would make certain she got the finest medical care available.

I was not happy with the situation from the start. The attending physician "quit" on Friday nights to spend time with her kids. I personally called her at home and encountered her husband whose job it was to screen her calls. My call was brief, only informing her that I would be arranging for my Mother to be sent to a Trauma Center. I then used one of my medical connections to procure a bed for her at a large hospital in Elmira, N.Y., close to my home. My brother Joe agreed with my decision. I had previously left a message for Jean on her machine informing her of Mom's accident. In retrospect, I wish I had left it at that. Unfortunately, I made a second call to her at midnight. This was a mistake because that call changed my Mom's fate and our lives forever.

Saturday morning arrived and I made plans to meet Mom at St. Joe's Hospital in Elmira. I telephoned the Hornell Hospital and spoke to Dr. Sinno. I cannot divulge all the details of what transpired due to a legal agreement. The doctor was an ally of Jean and she did not want my Mom moved near me. As a matter of fact, that very morning in my absence she had Mom sign a new Health Care Proxy to replace the one my Mom and I had established previously. I guess she felt since she was a nurse she would take over. I was livid, furious, and enraged! Sandy and I were forced to drive to Hornell to see what was happening. Jean didn't want my Mom moved near my home. It was only an hour away and we had an excellent trauma hospital. I could not believe this was happening! Everything that followed was not in my Mom's best interest. Sandy and I were powerless as "Nurse Jean" had put herself in charge and the local hospital and doctors welcomed her interference since they needed their empty beds filled.

I sat by each day watching my beloved Mother's health deteriorate before my eyes. I still agonize over the question, "Oh God, why didn't I fight harder to put my original plan into action?" The past week was hell, but it was nothing compared to what awaited us. Mom was transferred to a Clifton Springs Hospital for angioplasty. When she arrived, she was not in good condition and she was scared. Jean, even though she was a nurse, apparently did not recognize this and allowed her to continue with the angioplasty. I took an immediate dislike to the physician, but said nothing to stop the procedure. At this point I knew I lacked the medical expertise to make a decision. Halfway through the angioplasty, I alone was summoned to the operating room. Mom wanted to see me. What followed haunts me to this day and will continue to haunt me until the day I die. Mom was very weak but whispered in my ear, "Yanko, they are killing me. I don't want to die. I still want to see my grandchildren."

I then made the second mistake, a decision that I have difficulty living with. I allowed the procedure to continue thinking that I was doing what was best for my Mom. When my Mom returned from the operating room, she was unconscious and on a respirator. We were adamant that my Mom would not be returned to the Hornell Hospital and hoped that it was not too late for one of the Rochester City Hospitals to help her. Upon arrival at Rochester General Hospital, we were asked, "Why wasn't she sent here a week ago?" This confirmed what I had said from the start; Mom belonged at a Trauma Center from the first day of the accident. By now, more than a week had passed and our family kept a daily vigil at her bedside. We talked to her not knowing if she heard us or not. I suspect she understood we were there. We had hope that she would get through this. Mother's Day was approaching and I felt perhaps that we would get our miracle then. Instead, my Mother, Julia Katsur, former "Mother of the Year" died.

"Why? Why?" I sobbed. "Why on Mother's Day?" For the rest of our lives, Mother's Day would be a painful reminder of my Mother's death. Eventually, I adjusted my thinking and now believe that there is no better way to honor a "Mother of the Year" than to bring her home to God on this special day.

The days that followed were painful. Losing Mom was, in many ways, more difficult than any of the other deaths I had faced. There was so much to do to settle this estate and I knew it would all be left for me to do alone. I spent many hours sorting through personal belongings all representing a segment of my Mother's life. Many times tears would roll down my cheeks or else I would openly sob when I uncovered an item such as the picture I gave her in 1st grade that read "Mother I love you because you are so good to me." It took me months to fill four huge dumpsters. I had to arrange for the sale of the house as well as an estate sale. As far as disposition of my Mom's estate among her children, we had no problems. Mom would have been proud of the lack of squabbling. It took over a year to get things "buttoned up." I enjoyed keeping the lawn mowed and other odd jobs because it was the last time I would do something for my Mother. I am sure that my Mom knew everything would be done properly. In the end, I sold the house myself. I walked through every empty room in that house and cried in each of them. I thought of all the happy times spent there and knew this place would no longer be a part of our lives.

There was only one issue remaining — Mom had not died from her automobile accident injuries, and those individuals that caused her death must be held responsible. Malpractice is not about money, but about holding professionals responsible. I came to realize that doctors are not God, and that some do not deserve to work in their profession. My only desire was to confront these individuals eye to eye. Our hope was to prevent what happened to Mom from happening to someone else's mother. Our litigation was successful. In the end, we found peace and closure, but our actions could not bring my Mom back.

Chapter 42

DEBBIE'S WEDDING, JEFF'S CHALLENGE

Sandy and I spent several years enjoying Jeff after Johnny and Debbie were out on their own. It was a satisfying feeling. Deb had obtained her undergraduate and graduate degrees. In the late 1990's, we chased around with her from jobs as a guidance counselor in Presque Isle, Maine to Decatur, Illinois. We were able to enjoy her wedding in 1997. It was a great time. Don was a wonderful young man with a bright future. Both Johnny and Jeff were part of the wedding party. They used twin '55 Chevys to carry the wedding party. The wedding itself consisted of a Mass where serious consideration was given to the scripture readings. We were fortunate to have been able to provide a beautiful and enjoyable reception for our only daughter. The only cloud over the wedding was the presence of my sister and her daughter. They were unhappy because Don and Deb had chosen to have an adult wedding reception. They wanted them to change their wedding plans to accommodate my niece's children.

Sandy and I decided it was not fair to ask Don and Deb to do this since this was their special day. Consequently, both mother and daughter departed the reception early, but not before they made crude remarks pertaining to the food and so forth.

Only a few weeks prior to the wedding, our entire family flew to Louisiana to see Johnny receive his degree from McNeese University. He was now free to do what he wanted. We knew he was a survivor and would find his place in this world.

Nine and a half years had passed and we almost had the agency paid for. We were looking forward to freeing ourselves of this large debt. In the last six months, Bob told me he was getting back in the insurance business. I was surprised to say the least! He got a job at Prudential Insurance. He told me not to be concerned because he would never do anything to hurt my business. Bob eventually discussed working at our agency. I now had a completely new staff. I had no objection to him working with us, however he eventually began working for a competitor when our covenant expired. Sandy and I were hurt. Eventually, the situation grew better and Bob and I have a friendly relationship today.

Jeff had a turbulent high school career. Young people had changed so much since my two older children were in school. There seemed to be a lack of respect for authority. Smoking and drinking were on the rise. When the bell rang at the day's end, the teachers were out of there. We were concerned about Jeff because he seemed so sad at times. I prayed for guidance and one day in 1997 we made the decision to send him to Notre Dame, a Catholic High School. It had to be difficult for him entering a new school. It was not easy for us either. He rode to school with friends, but we often had to pick him up after school and then drive back for play practices, dances, and so forth. It was a fifty-mile round trip. Jeff made friends, mostly with the girls. He was kind and gentle and did not like people acting "macho." I believe his year at Notre Dame was good for him.

The summer prior to his Junior year, he told me Odessa was his school and where he belonged. Sandy and I agreed to let him start his Junior year there. He made some good friends with both boys and girls. He played soccer and was a standout on the swim team. His swim coach pushed the team hard, but Jeff endured. The pressures of competition weighed heavily on him. He would actually vomit between events and developed irritable bowel syndrome.

Jeff injured his knee that year and the orthopedic doctor did not allow him to finish the season. During the finals, the coach called me and said they needed Jeff back on the team because he was the best in the 100m butterfly. I explained that the doctor felt his knee was not healed and to return to competition could permanently disable him. Apparently, the coach was not happy with that response because at the Sports Boosters Dinner he presented picture plaques to everyone except Jeff. It was a cruel thing for the coach to do.

The next swim season, the coach waited for Jeff to swim, but Jeff decided against it. He was sure to get local and regional recognition, and Sandy and I wanted him to get the awards he deserved, but Jeff could care less. "Dad, in five years, I won't even know where those trophies are."

He enjoyed his senior year as an acclaimed art student, had the male lead in the musical, and was in the King's Court on prom night. At graduation, he received several awards and gave several moving speeches for retiring teachers. I was proud to give the Commencement speech that year, especially since the graduates themselves chose the speaker.

Chapter 43

REMINDER OF OUR MORTALITY

One of the things I did around that time was drink coffee at Teemley's Market. Sometimes as many as six or eight of us would sneak in the backdoor for coffee and chatter. Most of the guys were retired cops. We naturally would pick on one another, tell jokes, get the latest news, or solve the world's problems. Sandy had been out of town and I had not felt well. I had pains in my chest that I had been experiencing for about a week.

On this particular day when I drove to Teemley's for coffee, several of the guys mentioned that I was unusually quiet. Shortly after, the chest pains began. Walt, a retired New York City cop, looked at me and said, "Are you OK? You don't look good." I told him I was having chest pains and he asked if I wanted to go to the hospital. At first I said no, but I quickly changed my mind. The closer we got to the hospital, the more scared I became. I needed to get help desperately. Al Bulkley, a retired New York State Police Investigator and one of my closest friends, had gone to get Sandy. As they pushed me into the ER they began EKG tests. "Oh no! This can't be happening to me," I thought. "I don't have time for this!" My physician began discussing things like angioplasty that caused me to shudder.

Soon after this, a nurse put something into my mouth and I began to pass out.

I later learned that I had an allergic reaction to nitroglycerin. I truly believed at that moment that I was dying. My blood pressure dropped to fifty and I went into shock. They elevated my legs as my eyes spotted Sandy, Walt, and Al. Walt had a sad look in his eyes, which to me substantiated that I was indeed dying. I didn't have time for this. I couldn't believe that I woke up this morning, put on my shirt, tie, and suit, and started a normal day in all respects, and then two hours later, I felt like I'm dying. My thoughts were with my son Jeff because he still needed me and I still had work to do. I'm not ready to die. These were the various thoughts that ran through my head.

Shortly thereafter, I began to feel better. People were talking to me, but I was silent. I was digesting everything that had just happened to me. I was moved into intensive care and had plenty of time to contemplate the day's events and to reconstruct my priorities in life. Preliminary tests indicated that I had not had a heart attack. I was given a stress test the next day and told to go to Robert Packer Hospital for additional testing to determine if I had blocked arteries.

Before I could make an appointment, I received word that my good friend John Hubric had died. After a gallant, seven-year battle with cancer, he was gone. I had learned so much about living by watching John die slowly. He had taught me what was important in life, that real men were strong enough to express their emotions. At first, I was uncomfortable when he would say, "I love you, Bud," but I learned to say, "I love you too." Some of our fondest memories were spent with John, Bev, and their family. Our whole family would fly to Florida for Easter, Thanksgiving, or a birthday. On John's fiftieth birthday, Sandy and I flew down just for the weekend. Now he was gone and I wasn't sure if it was medically permissible for me to travel to Florida for the funeral. I wanted to go, and I did. Chuck Schwarz and I gave a moving eulogy that left us both emotionally drained.

Upon my return, I scheduled an appointment at Robert Packer Hospital for a Thelium Stress Test and MRI's. When I went for my follow up exam, the doctor said, "You are clean as a whistle. You have a greater chance of getting struck by lightning than having a heart attack." I continued to have severe chest pains that would usually manifest themselves at bedtime. The good news was that I knew I wasn't having a coronary, yet the pains continued each night. Sandy and I accepted Chuck and Gail Schwarz's invitation to join them at their condo on Hilton Head Island. Maybe the rest would do me good. As we walked the beach, I'd get sharp pains in my chest and I'd have to stop and rest until they went away. Sandy, my doctors, and I had no idea what was causing this so it was determined that stress was the culprit. I was now fifty years old. I was born into a stressful situation that seemed to follow me throughout my life.

Chapter 44

REVELATIONS OF REALITY

During the time our children were growing I was overly protective. If they were late, I'd picture them dead in a ditch. If I lost sight of Jeff at the mall, I figured he was kidnapped. In addition, I regimented our lives. Friday night the cars got washed, Saturday morning the lawns were mowed. When I gave an order, I expected that it would be carried out. If someone was late for anything, I'd fly into a rage. I was often not pleasant to be around and didn't know why. Family members stayed out of my way when I was in one of my "moods." It wasn't until Father's Day of 1996 that Johnny and I had a "blowout" and he said, "Dad you need help. You have a problem. There is no reason for you to get as upset as you do."

Someone finally stood up to me and I listened. I had heard the term "Vietnam Syndrome" and "Post-Traumatic Stress Disorder," but that wasn't me, was it? I mustered the courage to call the NYS Department of Veterans Affairs Office and asked the counselor if I could have PTSD. He felt that by virtue of the fact that I picked up the telephone and called him, I should go to a VA Hospital to be tested. I was confident that I did not have PTSD. I didn't wear camo and crawl around in my lawn at night with a bayonet in my teeth! I would submit to these tests to rule PTSD out just as I took all the tests at Robert Packer to rule out heart disease.

My first meeting with Dr. Q. was brief. He had received my (DD214) military discharge form and asked me a few questions before taking me to a room the size of a closet. There was a computer and a chair in the room. I learned the exam would take about two hours. It consisted of hundreds of questions about my feelings, thoughts, and actions. You could not fool the test; it was designed to ask the same question several times in different ways. If a patient gave the answer he or she thought was the correct response rather than the true response, it would become obvious. I was determined to answer the questions as honestly as I could. I needed to determine what my problem was and I fully expected to rule out Post-Traumatic Stress Disorder.

I waited about two weeks and eventually got a call from the VA Center requesting that I meet with Doc Quirion. Dr. Q. was a short, bearded man, and a former Air Force Officer who had a genuine concern for his patients. As I sat across from him, he again reviewed the tests that I had taken and stated that I tested very high for PTSD. I was surprised. He went on to explain that I was not crazy. "Had you gone through the horrors of combat and not been affected, then you would be nuts," he said. He went on to talk about how young we Vietnam Veterans were when we went to war. Most of us had been in high school a year or two earlier. "You, John, came home and buried the past. You created a normal life for yourself, getting married, raising a family, working, paying on a mortgage. You tried to move on." As he spoke, tears swelled up in my eyes.

For the first time since Vietnam, someone was telling me the rage I felt was not my fault. I thought I was just a "son of a bitch," but now I knew that there was a clinical reason for being this way. This diagnosis was both a beginning and an end for me. It was the end of a difficult existence and the beginning of learning about PTSD and trying to change who I was for the betterment of those around me. I learned that I was not alone, that many Vietnam Veterans suffered from PTSD. No one knew what PTSD was until the mid to late 1970's. Apparently I was a different breed of Nam Vet that was just coming "out of the closet" so to speak. The new breed blended into society. They did not wear camouflaged fatigues, but rather business suits. They were not drug users and in no way fit society's stereotype image of a Vietnam combat Veteran as described by the media.

The "new breeds" were doctors, attorneys, school teachers, and other productive members of society. Most of us had families, served on school boards, and were contributing members of our communities. Many were financially successful. The theory was that we buried the past and moved on. As we grew older, our children became adults, the house was paid for, and the college tuition was dispensed with. As our responsibilities in general diminished, we had more time to reflect upon the past. In some cases, the death of a parent or spouse could have "triggered" the return to the past.

Although I had no "flashbacks" per se, I did have exaggerated emotional and physical reactions to reminders of my Vietnam combat experience. The sound of a helicopter stopped me in my tracks. Whenever I heard one, I would stare at it silently, unaware of those around me. I would picture myself on an eagle flight into a mission or landing in an enemy stronghold. Likewise, a swamp would mesmerize me to the point that I would stop my car and stare at it. Chills would go up my spine as I envisioned myself wading through the water with only my head protruding. On a hot day after working in the yard, I would relish the taste of cold water and remember how thirsty I would get while on patrols in the jungle. Occasionally, I would have a dream where I was back in Vietnam and could even smell the place. A loud noise would send me looking for cover and make my heart pound. My children used to think it was a joke when they frightened me. They didn't understand; they thought I was being funny. Sandy saw no humor in me reacting by swinging my fists when startled.

I never fully understood the hyper-vigilance until one weekend when Sandy visited my Aunt. I was home alone and as darkness arrived, I became frightened. Every sound caused me to imagine danger lurking in the shadows. When I awoke in the morning, I noticed that I had my loaded revolver on the bed stand next to me. Staring at the pistol lying there scared me. Our house was carpeted and my hearing was damaged, but I could "sense" when our cat wandered into our bedroom at night. I jumped up from a deep sleep.

One of the more difficult symptoms of Post-Traumatic Stress was the emotional numbness that I possessed. I was not able to get close to people or express my emotions the way most people could. This was particularly difficult for my wife since she wanted to know and hear that she was loved and needed. Distrust was another sign of the disorder. In my own case, there were very few people I trusted. I always had to analyze situations. I felt like my mind played games with me. I would panic until my panic turned to anger and my anger turned to outright rage. I would become verbally abusive and hurt the ones I loved most with my words. Eventually, I would calm down and become remorseful, but the damage had already been inflicted. Exposure to Asians had an adverse effect on me as well. I would feel angry and defensive around them. As hard as I tried to avoid staring, I couldn't help it and would again become mesmerized by them. Sometimes I'd see them as VC, or peasants, or "boom boom" girls.

I began my therapy by meeting with Dr. Quirion every two weeks. We would discuss PTSD and he would ask me questions, allowing me time to say what was on my mind. Since I had never really talked about Vietnam to many people, this was an emotional topic for me. I would frequently feel tears falling from my eyes. One thing that continued to haunt me was the ages of the men fighting in Nam. We had been mere boys. Looking back on pictures in 1968, we looked like school kids. Jeff, Johnny and Debbie were all older than I was when I served in Nam. I knew that my comrades and I had lost something — our youth and our innocence. I was saddened by that knowledge and mourned the loss. My deepest regret was that my children would never know the "me" before Vietnam. I had been a "happy go lucky" fun loving teenager. I seldom got uptight and was always happy and laughing. Years later, a colleague described me as the most serious person he knew. That description both surprised and disturbed me.

Dr Q. stated that I had lost my ability to relax, and that this ability had been lost for over thirty years. I would return home after these sessions with newfound revelations. My family would chuckle and say, "We could have told you that, Dad." I suspect they knew me even better than I knew myself. Dr. Q. taught me methods of relaxing and ways in which to defuse my approaching rage. He performed hypnosis on me as a way to help me begin to relax and taught me self-hypnosis. Eventually I felt it was time to tell others about my diagnosis and treatment. It was particularly important that those who had experienced my rage be told. I sent letters and a VA brochure to Sandy's parents, my sister, my brothers, and to my children. I explained that this was in no way an excuse for my past behavior, but it was an "explanation."

Chapter 45

CONFRONTING VIETNAM PTSD

In addition to seeing Dr. Quirion the psychologist, I decided to avail myself of the services of Dr. Roe, the VA psychiatrist. To me, Dr. Roe was a strange woman. She was tall and thin, had short hair and spoke in a deep, gruff voice. She was direct and honest, and I liked her. She explained that there were two treatment theories regarding PTSD, psychological and physiological. Dr. Q. treated PTSD with counseling, hypnosis and so forth while Dr. Roe believed chemicals were the cause. Her theory was that the chemicals that were produced in the brain during extreme danger were still being produced. In essence, the spicket never got turned off. Since chemicals were the culprits, drugs were used to treat patients. I was not interested in taking medication. I did, however, continue to see her.

One of the subjects we discussed was my disciplined and regimented lifestyle, which was both a blessing and a curse. A blessing in the sense that I was goal oriented and could plan my work and then work my plan. It enabled me to become an effective manager. On the other hand, it was a curse because I made my family live by these same standards. If things didn't go according to schedule there was "hell to pay." Dr. Roe asked me,

"What did you do with your lawn if it was raining on Friday noon." I thought about that and replied, "Well, of course, I wouldn't mow." No, that wasn't the truth. I realized that I would even mow in the rain rather than disrupt my plan! Dr. Roe felt I might be depressed, but I wasn't buying it. There were times I would feel "down" and "crawl up inside myself," but I considered that normal. I would be quiet and non-communicative for a few days, but would kick myself in the ass and move on.

One of Dr. Q.'s treatments was REM or Rapid Eye Movement. The patient would move his eyes as the therapist would move his finger in various directions. This procedure was supposed to "unlock" suppressed memories in the brain. Dr. Q. told me to keep a note pad and pen near my bed as I might have "dreams" as a result of the REM treatment. He wanted me to write down the substance of these dreams. Again, I was a skeptic. As a matter of fact, I never even mentioned the procedure to Sandy. The first night nothing happened, but the following evening as I entered a deep sleep, I began to dream. The dream was not a combat type scene.

I remember being on a dock over some slimy green water. I told the men with me not to fall in the water because I would not go into the water to help them out. One of them deliberately jumped into the swamp like water and without hesitation I jumped in and pulled him out. We then were walking through a "rough" neighborhood when some men confronted us. They accused us of vandalizing their car. I tried to explain to them that we wouldn't do something like that and went on to explain that we were Vietnam Veterans, thinking that would help our cause. As soon as I said Vietnam Veterans, I consciously realized that this dream was related to the REM therapy. I understood that even though I was in a deep sleep, in the dream the situation worsened because of my comment. The men began to chase us and were throwing hand grenades at us and shooting at us. I remember running into a dilapidated house, up the stairs and into my bedroom. I grabbed a rifle, went out, and killed the man who had been chasing us. I then awoke from the dream.

It was about 3 a.m. and I ran into the kitchen for a pen and paper. I began to write furiously. Sandy looked at me, half-awake, wondering what was happening. When I was finished writing I began to tell her about the treatment at the VA hospital. She then asked me to tell her about my dream. "What's that noise," she asked. It was my heart beating. I was so scared from the dream encounter that my heart was racing as if I'd just competed in a marathon. I read the notes I had hurriedly scribbled. When I got to the part about killing the man, I began to cry. I sobbed uncontrollably. I could not stop crying. I cried and cried. I then proceeded to tell Sandy about Vietnam.

I had always been proud of my service, but at this moment I wished I'd never heard of Vietnam because of what it did indirectly to my wife and children. I felt that I would have been a better husband and father had I not experienced the horrors of war that resulted in this disorder. Oh, how I wished that I had not subjected my loved ones to the attributes of a post-traumatic personality! I felt so remorseful for my actions over the years! I told Sandy that she was a saint for having stuck by me. I have not been an easy man to live with and I doubted that anyone else could have persevered. She held me for several hours while thirty years of penned up emotion poured out. When it was over, I felt like a weight had been lifted from my shoulders. I was also afraid to go to sleep again for fear that I would have a recurrent dream.

I called Dr. Q. and discussed my experience asking if this was the result of the Rapid Eye Movement. He assured me that it was. He was not as interested in the substance of the dream as he was my reaction to it. I had a couple of dreams after that night. They were not as intense but followed the same theme. Someone was always trying to kill me and it usually was in a foreign land or by a foreign speaking person. For the first time, I began to believe there was a legitimate disorder called PTSD and perhaps there was treatment for it.

I did not hide my PTSD and shared the information with other Vets. Jay Voorhees has been my friend since the age of four. Although he moved away in the 4th grade, our lives intermittently crossed. Ironically, he went into the Army three days after I did. We trained at Ft. Dix at the same time although it wasn't until I got home from Vietnam that my Dad told me Jay was in Vietnam too.

We spent some time together after our discharges. Jay even attended Sandy and my wedding. We then lost track of one another for ten or fifteen years. On the way to the VA hospital, I stopped at his construction office. When he asked why I was going to the VA, I told him about the PTSD. He seemed interested. Eventually, we became reacquainted and would often meet for dinner with our wives.

Jay was always quizzing me about the PTSD and I openly shared information about some of the treatments, as they were interesting to most people. Finally, I said, "Jay, you are very interested in PTSD. Do you have a problem?" He confided that he might and I told him how to get tested.

There was another Vet in the community named Dale. He served time performing hazardous duty on a river patrol boat in the Mekong Delta. Dale had a real "attitude" about the military and the government. I suggested that he should go to the VA. His response was that he wanted nothing to do with the F-----g government. Dale seemed to get increasingly despondent and I heard he had made some comment about blowing his head off. I made a point of cornering him one day and told him that *I* had a problem. He listened as I explained what Post-Traumatic Stress was and how it affected combat Veterans. I knew Dale respected me and he was surprised that a successful business owner like myself could have problems. I ended our conversation saying, "If I can have war related problems, then you can too," and again offered to take him to the VA hospital with me. It was about two weeks later that Dale asked me to take him to the VA at my next visit. He was diagnosed with both physical and mental health problems and was placed in a treatment program. His wife has thanked me many times for getting him the help he needed, as it has made a tremendous difference in their lives.

I continued seeing Dr. Quirion and the VA "shrinks" who changed constantly. I was given Buspar for anxiety but nothing more. Eventually Dr. Q. started a PTSD therapy group. There were about a dozen of us in the group, mainly Marines but some Navy and Air Force Vets as well as a few Army "grunts," including my old friend Jay and myself. All of the group participants were decent men. They had wives, children, and good jobs. Some were divorced and for some reason several were postal workers. Each of us had a story to tell, unique to ourselves, yet we all shared a common experience and were suffering from many of the same symptoms.

Chapter 46

HONOR AT ARKPORT

At some point during my PTSD treatment, I began to think about Arkport, the community where I grew up. My life in the quiet village had been a good one. My memories were pure and wholesome ones. The people treated me with respect and dignity upon my return home and their welcome was sincere. I wanted to show my thanks in some way. I wrote a letter to my longtime friend Danny Hartwell in Arkport. I explained how I felt and told him that I would like to bring the replica of the Vietnam Memorial to Arkport. The following day I received a telephone call from Danny who had been considering this idea as well. We spoke at length about it and decided to enlist the help of the local American Legion Post. Eventually not only the Legion, but also several other groups within the Community got involved. We decided to coordinate the Vietnam Wall with the Village's annual "Summer Fest" and with a rededication of the Fred E. Kemp Little League Field named in honor of our childhood friend killed at Quang Tri Province in 1968. Although I had been away from the Community for more than thirty years, it seemed as though I had never left. It was more than a two-hour round trip drive for me to attend the planning meetings, but I looked forward to them. I met new people and got reacquainted with old friends.

Colleen Weekly, who had been my 4th grade teacher, was actively involved. She almost single handedly put together a book about the local boys who served in Vietnam. She even had two sets of post cards made. One was with Freddy Kemp's picture on it; the other had the High School yearbook pictures of all the Vietnam Veterans. The Post Office even did a commemorative stamp for that special day. Larry Jones, the supermarket owner and a prominent businessman, agreed to emcee the event. Larry had been just a child when we older boys went off to war.

I was able to get Jack Howe, a Vietnam Marine Vet; "Bing" the barber's son; and Greg Hollister, a recently retired Air Force Colonel, to speak. Greg had gone to school with my brother Bob and was too young for Vietnam, but he had a special place in his heart for Fred Kemp and for Vietnam Veterans as a whole. We had local, county, and state politicians there and I was honored to be able to take part in the program as well. I told no one about the battle I was having with PTSD. In my mind, this would be a test of how well I could handle the past. The planning of this event was a labor of love not only for Dan and I, but also for everyone involved. The feeling spread beyond the Village of Arkport to surrounding Communities and throughout Western New York. Anyone whose life had been touched by Vietnam saw this as an opportunity to come together after more than thirty years. It was a healing experience and probably one of the highlights of my life. The "Wall" was to arrive in July, however, that Memorial Day I was asked to return to Arkport to give the Memorial Day address. I carefully planned my speech. I wanted it to be from my heart. I didn't think I would have any difficulty giving the speech.

Chapter 47

MEMORIAL DAY OF ANGUISH AND HEALING

Memorial Day arrived and Sandy dropped me off at the school. The parade began there. I spotted Janice Ludwig's car marked "Gold Star Mother." I still had a problem confronting her. The clinical term was "Survivor's Guilt." I decided it was time to face my demons. I walked over to Janice's car. When I told her who I was she became excited and commented about how handsome I was. While blushing, I thanked her and told her that I was the speaker and would be mentioning her son Freddy in my speech. I rode in a different car in the parade and enjoyed seeing so many local families. When we arrived at the cemetery, Janice and I walked together to Freddy's grave where she began to talk about everything that happened. I was empathetic and sensed how difficult the years had been dealing with the loss of her son.

There was a large crowd there for the ceremony along with the Arkport Central School band. As I spoke, I became more and more emotional. It was not just about the war, but about returning to a place that I loved, a place filled with old friends and good memories. Somehow I got through the service and found it to be a rewarding experience.

Danny's wife LuAnn knew Memorial Day was difficult for me and questioned whether I'd be able to speak again for the Vietnam Wall Ceremony. I didn't know, but before long I'd find out. The preparations to get the Wall to Arkport were made. Leo Karr and Marty Davis, two retired Korean War Vets, volunteered to drive to Indiana to trailer it back to Arkport. Danny Hartwell and his crew did a fantastic job assembling the Wall and landscaping the area around it. They even had it lit at night. A tent was set up near it to assist the public in learning more about Vietnam, the Wall, and to help them locate the name of a friend or loved one. The weather that weekend was hot and sunny, perfect for the Summerfest. Saturday included not only the tribute to Vietnam Veterans but also the rededication of the Fred E. Kemp Memorial Field.

We had a crowd of several thousand there. Actually, over 10,000 people visited the Wall that weekend. The people really wanted to know about Vietnam and to talk with the Veterans. It was one of the biggest events to touch the Arkport community in a long time. Young and old came to share their thoughts. A spiritual healing occurred that weekend. I was pleased that Bev Hubric, Chuck Schwarz, and Dorenda Buisch came in from Florida, Massachusetts, and Michigan to support the ceremony and hear my speech.

When my turn came to address the crowd, I realized this would not be easy. It was as if time stood still. It's been said, "Time heals nothing. It's what is done with time that heals." Thirty years had not healed my wounds. Talking about the Vietnam War and listening to other Vets such as Jack Howe was emotionally draining. Many suppressed memories surfaced. I was glad that my speech was not as personal as it could have been, or I don't think I would have gotten through it. As part of the ceremony, we had the local Vietnam Veterans walk onto the field. They entered to the applause of the audience. The Vets told me that for the first time since they returned from Vietnam, they were proud of their service.

Having accomplished this goal, I returned to my normal life of managing the agency and being a husband and father. I continued to attend my therapy sessions at the VA Hospital.

Sandy and I got involved in two major projects in the summer of 1999. It had been our dream for many years to develop some land that we purchased from my Dad early in our marriage. We built a small pond and a barn on it. We now wanted to build a large pond covering five acres. It would be a major project and an expensive one. Our plan was to do things one step at a time, clear the trees one year and start construction later.

Chapter 48

ENVIRONMENTAL FOOLS

I wanted to do things correctly to avoid any problems with the State DEC. All of the locals advised me to just build it and not bother with permits. I gave that serious consideration, but in the end we decided to do things the right way to avoid problems. I called Dave Dupont at the U.S. Department of Agriculture's Soil and Water Division. Dave visited our site and studied the State Wetland maps before assuring us that it was okay to clear the site. The following year we hired Tom Hager, an engineer, and applied for all of the appropriate DEC permits. We waited for several weeks and finally I called DEC. When I asked about the permit, I was told that my permit was denied because I was in the Wetlands.

"What do you mean I'm in the Wetlands," I asked. "I was told that I was not in the Wetlands. I even have a letter for proof of that."

"Who sent you such a letter?" the bureaucrat asked.

"The Feds," I responded.

"Well we have jurisdiction over the Feds," he responded smugly.

It was decided that we'd all meet at the site on Tuesday. Dave Brimer and Scott Janes met with Dave Dupont and myself. In my opinion, Brimer was a decent man, but Janes rubbed us the wrong way from the start. As he looked at the site Scott said, "It looks like wetland." Then he sniffed his nose and said that it smelled like wetlands too. We all stared at him in amazement: I said, "Scott, of course, it looks like wetlands. When we cleared the forest, we changed the seedbed and this is the new vegetation. This was not what was here last year." He then got a "smirk" on his face and started describing the type of pond he would like. When he finished, I said, "Scott, why don't you build the type of pond you want for your family and I'll build the type I want for mine." That really upset him. I tried to pacify him, but the damage had already been done.

I couldn't believe that some wet-behind-the-ears bureaucrat was now telling me what to do with my land. My family had owned this land since 1939. For sixty years we paid taxes on this scrubland and no one paid one iota of attention to it. Suddenly this was the most important land on earth. I tried to explain that I wasn't filling in the wetlands — I was making it wetter. We had by now spent several thousand hard earned dollars on the project.

What was supposed to be a labor of love turned into a nightmare because of one man at DEC who was abusing his power. Normally, I would not have put up with this, but Dave Dupont urged me not to "pull my trigger." I agreed to mitigate the plan in order to proceed with construction. I put everything in writing and sent it to the DEC and advised them that if there was a problem, they could call me, otherwise we'd continue construction. We heard nothing until a DEC officer appeared at the site threatening to arrest us unless we stopped building the pond.

When I called Scott Janes he was rude and obnoxious. He said, "Mr. Senka, by law we have two weeks to respond to your letter." He went on to say that I had violated the law on two occasions and that he had now gotten the Army Corps of Engineers involved in my project. This spoke volumes about the man. He was vindictive. Eventually I spoke to Assemblyman

Jim Bacalles and within forty-eight hours, I had my permit. Unfortunately, it was too late. The wonderfully dry summer had turned into a wet autumn and the contractor could not continue the project until the following year. In the interim, we were left to look at a $25,000 mudhole.

Chapter 49

POST OFFICE CAPERS AND CUPID'S HELPER

That same autumn, I was approached to sell my office building to a developer who wanted to build a new Post Office. I was told that I had the prime location. I gave the idea serious thought, but discovered it would be impossible to find a decent new location and it was too expensive to rebuild. Sandy and I then educated ourselves on ownership of a Post Office. We discovered that being a landlord was an extremely lucrative proposition. We could expect close to $5,000 per month in rent with increases every five years for twenty years. It was an investment that would have provided a dignified retirement for Sandy and me. So we decided not to sell our property, but to demolish our office and to build a combination Post Office and new insurance office.

The other developer obtained an option on an inferior location near ours. Subsequently, a battle ensued that divided the Community. The majority of the local citizens favored my location and preferred that a local person be awarded the contract rather than an "out of towner." Our argument was that not only was my location better, but I had also supported the community, school, and various groups for close to twenty years, whereas an out-of-town developer had done nothing and he would make his money in our village only to spend it elsewhere. Small towns being what they are, there grew to be many petty jealousies. There were some people who didn't want to see a local person prosper, while others genuinely wanted to clean up the other property.

There were several meetings where citizens engaged in lively discussions. I was proud of the way my son John and his fiancée Tambi supported us and spoke on our behalf. Many friends, clients, and former employees also publicly supported us. The process was a long one and it would be months before we knew the outcome. In the interim, I continued working, serving on various community boards, and helping my kids. Time was a valuable commodity. These two projects were extremely stressful.

We had many good friends who we were able to spend time with. Dorenda Buisch, a girl I'd known since early childhood, had come back into our lives. She had been married for twenty-eight years and had gone through a divorce. I was able to lend moral support during that time and she became like part of our family. She became particularly close to our youngest son Jeff. Dorenda was an artist and Jeff flew to Traverse City, Michigan to spend time with her. Dorenda showed him the area and they painted together. Coincidentally, I had also gotten reacquainted with Greg Zimmer, my infamous friend from college. Greg had also just gone through a divorce. He owned a medical employment business in Rochester. I had introduced Greg and Dorenda back at Alfred State and again now. More than thirty years later, they had fallen in love.

Chapter 50

DEVELOPING STORMS

I continued seeing Dr. Quirion and made time for monthly group sessions. In addition, I occasionally saw a VA psychiatrist. This psychiatrist seemed much more astute than most of the other "shrinks" I had seen.

She asked, "How long have you been depressed?"

"I'm not depressed. Why do you think I'm depressed?"

She answered, "You look depressed. You should take Paxil."

"I really don't want to take any more meds,"

She replied, "Look, I'll prescribe Paxil. If you decide you don't need it, then dump them in the sink. I don't care."

She then asked me what I thought depression was. I knew that from time to time I would get "down," perhaps once or twice a year. I started taking half a Paxil each day and continued to enjoy life. My family told me I was much more pleasant to be around since I began therapy for Post-Traumatic Stress Disorder.

Sandy and I had been married thirty years and had been taking care of at least one of our children for twenty-nine of them. In 1999, Jeff prepared to leave for Fairmont State College in West Virginia. We had looked at several schools with him and Fairmont seemed to be the best fit. We missed Jeff and wondered why he had to go so far away, but we also realized he needed to grow up and not depend on us so much.

He seemed to be doing well at Fairmont. He was elected to the student senate, a significant honor for a freshman. He was also asked to pledge one of the top fraternities on campus. Jeff and his long-time girlfriend Kim had decided to go their separate ways; they knew they should both be free to date others.

One day he called me to tell me about a new love. Her name was Heather and she was deaf. This concerned me, but not Jeff. He had always been open to relationships and friendships with people that were different. It made no difference to him whether a person was fat or thin, black or white, tall or short, pretty or ugly. He judged others by the way they treated him and had almost a sixth sense about a person's character within minutes of meeting them.

Sandy and I were thoroughly enjoying our "empty nest." We would watch TV while we ate dinner and then relax in the hot tub or take a walk together. Sometimes we would visit other couples. Usually by 9 o'clock, we'd get into bed and read for an hour or so before falling asleep. It was a very satisfying lifestyle. It was about October that we received a call from Jeff. He did not sound like himself. He told us that he was tired and couldn't get to classes in the morning. We emphasized how important it was not to skip classes or he'd end up failing. I figured he'd do whatever it took to stay in college. Soon after, we received a call from his friend Ryan. Apparently, Jeff was now sleeping most of the time. He also had problems with his roommate and had moved out of the dorm and in with friends. His belongings were in his car. There had to be something drastically wrong! Could he have mono or a mental illness?

We could not resolve anything from New York, so Sandy and I drove to Fairmont, West Virginia. We found Jeff at the apartment of a young woman. It was later in the day and he was functioning quite well. We all went to his friend Ryan's apartment and later his friend Heather arrived. Heather was absolutely beautiful. She had blonde hair, blue eyes and a perfect complexion. Jeff, Heather, and their friends joined us for dinner. Throughout the evening Jeff and Heather spoke in sign language, oblivious to the rest of us. I wish I hadn't made an issue of her deafness. She was a lovely, personable young lady.

The next morning Jeff couldn't wake up again. Finally, about noon, we took him to the medical center for blood work. Our hope was that he had mono or some simple explanation for his condition. Earlier that day Sandy and I had visited every one of his professors. We wanted to explain his absence from classes. We explained that he was ill and was not just skipping classes. All of his professors were understanding and sympathetic to our situation. Jeff's blood tests were negative for mono or any other obvious disorder.

We could not leave Jeff there in his current living situation. Amy, one of the admission counselors with whom we had become friends, suggested we contact her former landlords. They were an older Italian couple that owned a family restaurant nearby. They had living quarters adjacent to the restaurant and had two apartments upstairs over the restaurant. They agreed to rent one of the apartments to Jeff. It was an attractive, clean place and he could eat his meals at their restaurant. The food was homemade and delicious. The only problem was that he needed furniture. We helped him move the bulk of his personal belongings into the new apartment. Sandy and I then drove back to New York stopping at our daughter Deb and son-in-law Don's home in State College, P.A. We explained the situation to them and they didn't hesitate to offer their help. We decided that the following weekend we would pack our Explorer and Don's pickup truck with a bed and other furnishings.

I spent the next few days trying to catch up on my work at the office. Before we knew it, we were headed back to West Virginia. We arrived on a Saturday morning and quickly began the tedious process of unloading the vehicles, carrying everything upstairs, and putting them in the proper place. It took us all day and we celebrated by going out to dinner. Jeff and his friends joined us again. We spent the night at the Holiday Inn and by Sunday morning we were ready for the long drive back to New York.

We were full of hope that Jeff would still be able to salvage his first semester of college. He would be home for Thanksgiving and we planned to get an appointment with a psychiatrist to determine if there was perhaps a psychological problem. Our carefree, empty-nest lifestyle had come to an end. Deb and Don were doing great. They had purchased a beautiful home in State College. Don's career was on the move and Deb enjoyed her work as a counselor at a center for abused women. Johnny had been working as a caseworker with foster children, but began a new career with Progressive Insurance as a claims adjuster. His girlfriend Tambi, with whom he lived, had a good job teaching art at two different schools.

I began to feel like I should have listened to Sandy when she wanted to stop with two children. Yet we both loved Jeff dearly and knew our lives were better because of him. These thoughts, however, continued to dwell in my mind. It was insane for God's sake; we'd had Jeff for eighteen years. Why was I imagining a scenario without him here? He was here and we had to help him deal with his problems.

Jeff arrived home for Thanksgiving and seemed much better. He spent time with his friends and got some of Sandy's home cooking. We met with Dr. Margo Fass, a psychiatrist that had been recommended to us. Dr. Fass was an artist, a Mother Earth-type woman, and rather "crunchy." She administered a battery of tests to Jeff and diagnosed him as highly depressed. She put him on medication.

Chapter 51

JEFF'S RECOVERY

Thanksgiving was over so we sent our son back to college. We hoped that the medicine would now allow him to successfully complete the semester. He had no more than arrived back at Fairmont when he called to tell us he was withdrawing from college and coming home. We were crushed; our plans and hopes for Jeff were shattered. We now had to drive to West Virginia and move all his furniture and belongings back home. Again, Don and Deb and Dorenda Buisch agreed to help us move Jeff back home. Those past weeks of worry, anxiety, and lack of rest, etc., took their toll on us. We were indebted to Don, Deb, and Dorenda for their help.

I was meeting with Dr. Q. at the VA Hospital and he was trying his best to help me deal with Jeff's situation. In addition, I was seeing a VA "shrink" myself. Dr. Enrico suggested I increase my meds. I was beginning to have more problems with the effects of my PTSD. Every morning when I awoke, I'd be thinking about Vietnam and reliving the events of 1968. Hank, Andy, Glenn, Truc and Schmid, all buddies who died in Nam became my constant companions. Wherever I was, they were with me. I could actually feel their presence.

221

I still carried a great deal of guilt as I tried to solve the complex puzzle as to why I lived and they died. I often would imagine some Vietnamese people disabled due to my actions, or wondered if some child had been raised without a father because of me. To further complicate matters, I began to react adversely towards Dr. Enrico. Whenever I saw this small oriental man, I would visualize him as a North Vietnamese officer. My body would almost separate into two parts as I would watch myself shooting him with my M16. I decided at that point to stop my visits with him.

We planned another long weekend to make the trip to West Virginia. We phoned ahead to ask Jeff to start packing, but it was obvious that he was not functioning. He was still in bed. When we finally arrived, the five of us, with limited help from Jeff, began packing and loading the SUV and truck. We stopped only to eat lunch and for Jeff to say goodbye to several friends that had stopped by. We turned around and headed back to New York that same day. Jeff drove himself home a couple days later.

Once home, we had to unload and put everything in storage. We were physically and mentally exhausted. I returned to work and tried to get caught up, but I was still thinking and worrying about my youngest son most of the time. When Jeff arrived home, the first thing we did was to arrange a consultation with Dr. Margo Fass. Her evaluation indicated that Jeff's depression was now almost non-existent. We couldn't believe that removing him from his environment could instill such a rapid recovery. Dr. Fass made a follow-up appointment with him for the middle of the following week.

We didn't want Jeff lying around doing nothing so we suggested that he either enroll at the local Community College or get a job. He apparently had enough of college at that point, so he applied for a job at McKenzie-Childs in Aurora, N.Y. Aurora was more than one and a half hours away. He had been fascinated with the place when he went there on a field trip for a high school art class. They produced and painted pottery by hand. When the day of his appointment with Dr. Fass arrived, he informed us that he had a job interview scheduled at McKenzie-Child. Sandy and I went to Dr. Fass's office without him.

When we arrived at her office and explained the situation, she said, "That doesn't surprise me." And then she said something that shocked me, "I'm not worried about your son. He'll be fine. It's you that concerns me." "Me?" I replied. "Yes. Have you ever seen a psychiatrist?" I then explained to her about my PTSD related to Vietnam. I learned that she worked for the VA at one time and was familiar with Post-Traumatic Stress Disorder. Apparently, she did not agree with or conform to the VA's method of treatment. She let me know that she had a clientele of Vietnam Vets whom she was treating for PTSD. I departed from her office that day feeling that we had probably seen the last of her. Jeff didn't need her and I was sure I didn't either. Little did I know what was in store for me.

Jeff started his job, getting up each day at 5:00 a.m. and taking the long drive to Aurora. We realized he surely had recovered from his depression, because otherwise he certainly wouldn't be rising at that ungodly hour.

Chapter 52

THE NIGHTMARE WITHIN

I was back to my daily routine at work. I remember one day sitting at my desk going through the daily mail. I suddenly felt "detached" from my business. It was as if I was no longer needed here and that I served no purpose. I felt useless. I had always enjoyed work and solving problems, meeting with clients, and interacting with my staff. I went home that night feeling lost and confused.

The next morning in early November of 1999, my nightmare began. I still am not sure what to call it. Acute clinical depression? Nervous breakdown? Or was it a spiritual journey? Perhaps I was experiencing something called the "Dark Night of the Soul." I lay in bed drenched in sweat. I was in the fetal position. I was scared. No, I was petrified! I began to sob. Sandy didn't know what to make of this. She spoke to me as I asked her to hold me.

"What's wrong," she asked.

"I'm afraid."

"Of what," she asked.

"I'm afraid of everything," was my response.

I was afraid of losing my business. I thought I would lose all I had worked for. I even visualized myself living on the street in a cardboard box. I was worried about Jeff, too. Fear and worry were the overwhelming emotions I was feeling. When Sandy prompted me to get out of bed, I couldn't. It was as if that bed and I were one.

Finally, by late morning, I had made it into the bathroom. That fifteen feet from my bed to the bathroom seemed like a climb up Mt. Everest. When I saw my face reflected in the mirror, I could hardly recognize myself. I just stood there staring at the face staring back at me. Who was this person? I did not know him. Trying to shave was a major chore. The razor felt so heavy and my hand was so unsteady. As I entered the shower, I shook and found it difficult to stand erect. The spray from the water hitting my body actually hurt. It felt as if needles were striking me. The simple routine of dressing myself became overwhelming to me. I no longer felt steady on my feet. It took me forever to get dressed and to get my shoes on my feet. I was not hungry, but took my Paxil and Buspar.

I felt funny arriving at work so late. I really don't remember if I offered any explanation to my fellow workers or not. Being in the office seemed to further upset me. Whenever my phone would ring, I would panic. No matter how simple a problem would be, I could not deal with it. I was also so tired. I found myself leaving the office periodically just to escape my surroundings. Most of the time I would go home and hug Sandy. I would seek reassurance from her that our lives would be okay.

At lunchtime, I discovered that I still had no appetite. I would lie down on the sofa, but could not sleep. I had no interest in watching the TV. As a matter of fact, the TV disturbed me. I would force myself back to the office, but was conspicuously quiet, not speaking to anyone. I would continue to return home throughout the day for reassurances from Sandy that we'd be okay. I was relieved when 5 o'clock came and I could go home. The first thing I would do is change into my pajamas and lie down.

I was starved at supper since I hadn't eaten all day. I gorged on the food. After dinner, I would read because the TV disturbed me. I would go to bed by 8 o'clock but I couldn't sleep. It would be 1 or 2 in the morning before I would finally fall asleep.

The next day was the same. I would awake hoping I was normal again, but I wasn't. I'd lay in the fetal position, wet from night sweats. It was impossible to get out of bed. When I finally did, I would run to the kitchen to get my meds. I felt like a junkie as my shaky hands would open the bottle and I would dump the pills down my throat in hopes of a quick fix. The whole routine of shaving, showering, and dressing would then start again. What is routine to most of us became an insurmountable effort for me.

As I entered my office around 10 or 11 a.m., the ladies wondered what my condition would be. It was quite obvious the second I entered the building that I was not better. In retrospect, it had to be an uneasy situation for Anne, Emily, and Challiss. I would try my best to function, but just being in the office building depressed me more. I would go out and shovel the snow, go to the Post Office, anything to get me out of there. Whenever my telephone rang, I'd jump, shake and become anxious. The simplest of tasks, such as a routine deer claim or broken windshield would seem catastrophic. If a client was upset or had a serious problem I couldn't deal with it. Eventually, the staff would "cover" for me or handle things themselves. This continued day after day, week after week.

By the first of each week, I would tell Sandy to make an appointment with the psychiatrist Dr. Fass. I needed help, I couldn't continue like this. How long would this last? Dr. Fass was good about getting me into her office. Sandy drove me to her office located in an old railroad depot overlooking Keuka Lake. Her practice involved three elements – physical, mental, and spiritual. I was desperate, and even though I perceived myself in financial ruin, I willingly shelled out the $120 per hour fee. At the end of each session, Dr. Fass would ask if I wanted to make an appointment for the following week and I would emphatically say no.

On the way to our car, Sandy asked why I didn't make an appointment and I'd tell her that I got little if anything out of the

227

session. I was spending $120 for nothing. Usually, before we had gotten five miles from her office on our return trip home, I would breakdown. So many thoughts would surface. Whether real or imagined, it was my perception and my reality. They usually pertained to what a "son of a bitch" I was. It seemed as if every "bad" thing I'd ever done surfaced in my mind. I told Sandy that I thought God was punishing me for being a bad person. I confessed that I had been wrong to alienate her parents all these years and perhaps that is why God took my parents from me. My folks spent more time with our children than hers did. Now her parents had the grandchildren to themselves. I told her how badly I felt about the way I treated her over the years. I was too dominant, too controlling, and too quick to anger. I could think of nothing good about myself. As I felt the pain that I had caused others and as I sobbed, I actually started to feel better. Letting go means you don't have to carry it around anymore.

To be critical of myself, let alone self-condemning, was not characteristic of me. My normally large ego was stripped from me. I looked forward to the weekend so I wouldn't have to force myself to get out of bed, let alone function. I stayed in bed until noon. After showering and dressing, I picked up the office mail and took it to the office. I became anxious the closer I got to the building and being inside, even though we were closed, bothered me.

I went home and stretched out on the couch, but could not sleep. I heard every gong of my many clocks. I literally listened to the next twenty-four hours pass. 1:00, 1:30, 2:00, 2:30, 7:00, 7:30 and so on. This went on the entire weekend. The following weeks were the same. One morning the bedside phone rang and I felt as if a bomb had exploded. I shook all over. I ripped the cord out. I could no longer tolerate the simple ringing of the telephone. Eventually, I asked Sandy not to play the television around me. I had no interest in TV and the sounds bothered me. We no longer played the radio or CD player in our cars.

As the weeks passed, I would awake each day hoping I was normal again, but I was not. I could no longer sleep in our bed. I hated that bed where I would sweat profusely and could not sleep. I told Sandy that I preferred to sleep alone and began searching for a new bed. Since we had three extra bedrooms, I tried each. I'd sleep downstairs for a few nights and then I'd try Johnny's old room. Nothing seemed to help, but I felt better than I did in my "marital bed."

Our social life stopped completely. We no longer went out to dinner or visited with friends. When a friend caught me at the wrong time, I openly explained what was happening. Almost everyone was shocked. I apparently was the last person anyone expected to be hit with acute depression. My friend Chuck Ciprich actually thought I looked "blue." Jay Voorhees, Bev Hubric, Chuck Schwarz, Dorenda and Greg, and others called me every few days to see how I was doing and to show their concern. I had to cut our conversations short. I would leave the house struggling to be positive and upbeat. I'd arrive at work and start fielding phone calls. By the time I explained the depression to all my concerned friends, I'd have dragged myself back down. Sandy finally suggested I thank each person for their concern and tell them I'd call when I felt better. Bev started sending me passages from the Bible, which I would read each evening. I was given medical books about depression, which I also read fervently.

Each week I'd continue seeing Dr. Fass and new revelations would appear. The doctor felt I had too much on my plate and suggested I eliminate all stress from my life. I began by resigning from all clubs and boards I belonged to. People who did not know what I was going through misinterpreted my motives. I agreed to serve my term on the IDA Board, but even that was a source of anxiety for me. Dr. Fass then advised me to retire. How could I retire? The only real retirement I had was what I was able to save and invest over the years. Considering that I had paid Johnny and Deb's college debt in full, helped them with cars, and paid for a wedding, we had done okay, but I still felt a financial responsibility to Jeff. No, retirement was not an option. What would I do? I don't like golf. I'd sit around and worry and really go nuts.

Disability was suggested, but when I called my partner in Olean, I discovered our health insurance coverage was limited. His attitude was "go on disability. It's a sweet deal." It wasn't a "sweet deal" and he showed little if any empathy towards my plight.

Dr. Fass increased my medications substantially. She felt the dosage given to me by the VA was like "peeing in the ocean." Each week I hoped would be my last, but by the next week I'd ask Sandy to make another appointment. Jeff was the only one who understood what was happening to me. He'd say, "Dad, I hate to see you this way, but now you know what I went through."

The depression was taking everything I enjoyed away from me. I no longer enjoyed food, and following the Stock Market on TV was my passion, but I no longer watched TV. I loved reading the newspaper but I would now take it out of the tube each morning and toss it in the trash. I wanted to cancel our subscription, but Sandy urged me not to. She said, "You won't be like this forever." I wasn't so sure. I always enjoyed my sleep, especially dozing off at noon in my chair, but now I'd forgotten what a good night's rest was like. Our sex life, which had been wonderful, was virtually non-existent. We didn't even sleep together. I even missed hearing my own voice. I usually sang along with the radio or CD player whenever we were in the car, but that too stopped. This continued week after week with no end in sight. Every day was a struggle.

We would occasionally visit with Lee and Penny Titus, close friends who I could talk with. Penny was a spiritual woman who had some insight to my struggle. Lee is a compassionate man and a good listener who seemed to have the right responses. I once confided to him that I had thoughts of going into the forest behind my house and using a shotgun to end my suffering. If I didn't have Sandy, I probably would. He calmly looked at me and said, "Well, then be glad you have Sandy."

Bill and Carol Peters forced us to get out once in a while. Bill was a competitor and we enjoyed each other's company and had become close friends. Carol is a compassionate woman. They would call us and invite us to go to a RV show, or shopping. It would be difficult for me to accept these invitations. It was easier to crawl up into a ball and vegetate at home, but I did it for Sandy. She was my "rock" and I knew she had to get out of the house. Usually after spending the day with Bill and Carol, perhaps having dinner out, I would feel better.

I began to hug the women for some reason. I can't explain why, but I had an overwhelming need to do this whenever we met or when we departed. Something about the physical closeness helped. I continued seeing Dr. Q. at the VA. By now, I constantly huffed. It was as if I was winded from physical activity. I also felt an emptiness within me that is hard to describe. It was like a hole in my heart. Dr. Fass said that it was a sign of grieving.

"What was I grieving for," I asked.

"A loss," she replied.

Sandy seemed to have some insight. "You are not the same person," she said. "Perhaps you are mourning the loss of you."

On one visit to Dr. Q., he stared at me blankly, "John, I am afraid for you."

"What do you mean," I replied.

"You don't look good. You are falling into a deep, dark pit and I'm concerned that we won't be able to get you out."

Chapter 53

SPIRITUAL SEARCHING

When I departed the VA Hospital that day, I drove directly to St. Anthony's at Padua. It had been a school and monastery owned by the Franciscans. There was now only one Franciscan priest who lived there. I parked my car and knocked on the front door. An elderly lady answered and I told her I had to see Father Austin. The priest was saying Mass in his chapel but soon appeared to welcome me. "Father, I need to go to confession." We walked into his chapel and I knelt down on the hard wooden kneelers. I confessed to everything I could think of past and current. I then tried to explain my PTSD problems from the war and my anxiety over Jeff.

Father listened and spoke to me. The main revelation was that I must understand that "God is in control. Not you, but God." I had to come to grips with this fact. It was true. My entire life I was able to make things happen and fix problems as they arose. This was a new concept for me. I understood it, but I was having difficulty accepting it. For penance, Father asked me to read the first chapter in a book on the life of St. Joseph We then returned to his kitchen and talked for another couple of hours. I was in awe of this intelligent, simple man who was so at peace with himself.

The fall holiday season was approaching. The weather turned cold and snow began to cover the countryside. My depression had gotten so bad that I now had to stop the many clocks in my house because the tick/tock and gongs made me more anxious than I already was. On the weekends I would lie on the sofa until I couldn't stand it and then I'd go out in zero degree weather and walk. It took all the energy I could muster to do this. I began to have more thoughts of suicide. At first, I would hope I wouldn't wake up tomorrow. One time I told Bev Hubric that I envied her husband John who had died of cancer a couple of years earlier.

Christmas was close but I wasn't enthused about it at all. Rita Banfi, a close friend from Arizona, was coming to visit. We called her to forewarn her what to expect to see when she got here. Anne, Emily, and Challis were "running things" and decorated the office to reflect the holiday season. I felt terribly guilty that I was not holding up my end, and I broke down a few times as I hugged each one.

One day I sent Sandy's folks a card telling them how important they were to my family and me and invited them to spend Christmas with us. Everything I did was honest and sincere. Ego no longer came into play and machismo was out the window. I was honest and sincere in all that I did and said. Sandy could not believe the change in me. My actions and words could not have been expressed or said prior to this depression. I felt as if I was "stripped naked" before the world. Sandy saw the change as positive and was enjoying, to some degree, the affection I was showing. I would hug her ten or fifteen times each day. She did not enjoy the negative side of this, especially the suicidal thoughts. She would often call me if I did not return home when expected. I knew she feared the worse. She described me to Dr. Fass as having a "Broken Spirit." I had once been a strong, confident "rock," but I had turned into a broken man who was afraid of everything, had no confidence and no sense of worth.

Although I was not enthused about Christmas, I did look forward to being out of the office for a few days. Sandy's folks, Louie and Florence, arrived Christmas Eve day and, for the first time, got a first-hand look at what had happened to me. I don't know how much Sandy had told them about my condition. I am certain seeing me like that had to be a real shocker. Our children started filtering in. Even though they were adults, they enjoyed returning to their old bedrooms for Christmas Eve.

Thanks to my sister's insistence that my parents spend all holidays at her house, she had inadvertently given my family a great gift. We had traditional holidays, enjoying one another. When my folks died, even though we missed them terribly, it did not adversely impact our holidays. Our Christmas' are wonderful primarily because of Sandy. She puts so much love and enthusiasm into the holidays. She decorates the entire home including the outdoor lighting. She bakes extensively, not only traditional cookies, but also delicate European Kolachki. We always attend family Mass and have pierogie afterward. I always light candles in memory of our deceased family members.

This Christmas Rita joined us for dinner. She and I always enjoyed drinking wine and lively conversation. This year I either sat quietly at the table or was stretched out on the sofa listening to the others in the dining room. Johnny had not arrived for dinner. I knew he had to work late, but had hoped he'd make it to Mass. I had concern about the religious and spiritual needs of my children. Sandy and I had done our best to bring them up in the Roman Catholic Church. I knew how important one's faith could be during difficult times. When he and Tambi finally arrived, I could see him glancing over at me waiting for me to blow my stack. It never happened, and I knew that perplexed him. He hadn't been around too much and didn't realize the extent of what was happening to me, or, if he did, he was uncomfortable seeing me like that. He found it easier to stay away. Shortly after dinner, I went to bed in our bedroom.

Christmas morning arrived and I found it impossible to get out of bed. The family wanted me to go downstairs to open gifts. This was always a special time for our family. I was the one who passed out each present and said who it was for and from whom it was given. We would then watch the recipient open their gift. Sandy always went overboard on the number of gifts so this process would take a long time, but we enjoyed it. On this morning, I offered to relinquish the presentation of gifts job to someone else, but they insisted I do it. Shortly after I got started, the phone rang and it was Russ Rose, my former boss at Met Life. Russ knew what I was going through and called to wish me a Merry Christmas and to offer words of encouragement.

I spent most of Christmas Day lying on the sofa. Debbie, who had a Masters degree in Psychology and Counseling, spent hours talking to me about my depression and offered me advice. This was certainly a role reversal. She explained that I had to feel whatever emotion I was feeling, whatever that emotion was, no matter how painful it was. "One must feel it to heal it." She also suggested I substitute the word "could" for "should." An example was I "should go" to the office versus I "could go" to the office.

Don also got involved in our discussions and appeared interested in hearing what I was experiencing and I expressed my feelings in total honesty. The depression had long disposed of a façade or charade on my part.

Christmas Day also brought me closer to my mother-in-law, Florence. I saw her and Louie in a different light. They were simple, God-fearing people who were thankful for what they had. I could see that they were at peace with themselves. I regretted deeply any hurt I had caused them. At one point, I asked Florence to pray for me and she said she had been for a long time. I took her into a room by ourselves and apologized for my past behavior and told her that I loved her. We both wept and she told me she had waited thirty years to hear that. As painful as this depression was, I was also discovering that there were blessings, too. How wonderful it was that I could make these amends before it had been too late. I hugged my children more and told them how much I loved them. I asked Sandy's folks to stay another day and to attend Church with us on Sunday.

Attending Church was not easy; I still could not awake on time. On this particular Sunday, we went to 11 a.m. Mass. I felt good being in Church. It had a whole new meaning for my life. I had never noticed how often the priest used words like "anxiety" and "peace of mind." In the past, these were just words, but now they meant something to me. Having "peace of mind" and being "free of anxiety" were truly gifts from God. I now knew first hand that without them life was not worth living. I began to feel closer to God and needed to learn more about Him. I began to read the Bible and other inspirational books. I read scripture and prayed continuously. Why was God allowing this to happen to me? There had to be a reason. Other Christians assured me that God was not punishing me. I learned about Job and how God had tested his faith by taking all that was dear to him. "I'm not as strong as Job," I thought. I knew this depression that had "broken me" could destroy me.

The holiday was ending and everyone was returning to their routine. Don, my son-in-law, said to me, "Thanks for a nice Christmas." I didn't know whether to laugh or cry. "Right," I said. "It must have been great listening to me these past few days," I said facetiously. Don became serious and said, "I've never been able to express my emotions. I was taught men don't cry. It wasn't until I met Debbie that I learned it was okay to express my feelings." He then said something that touched me deeply. "I really feel privileged to be a part of your family." Usually, whenever Don departed our home, he and I would shake hands, but on this day we hugged, and, before they left, the four of us encircled one another and said, "I love you." I invited Deb to my next therapy session with Dr. Fass because I thought it might be of interest to her and I wanted her opinion of the psychiatrist.

Chapter 54

MILLENNIUM CHALLENGE

The new millennium was now approaching. Most people were excited, but not me. What a way to end the century, or start a new one! It wouldn't have mattered to me if the world came to an end. As a matter of fact, I hoped it would. Weeks had passed since this struck me. I knew that for over fifty years I'd had good days. Days that I had taken for granted. Now I forgot what a good day was like. I actually had forgotten what it felt like to be "normal." I would walk through a busy store and stare at the people. I was envious that they were normal and I was not.

Sandy and I had spent the past several New Year's Eves with Bill and Carol Peters. It was usually a quiet evening where Bill and I enjoyed eating crab, lobster, and steak. Sandy and I always looked forward to it. This year, as much as I wanted to enjoy the evening, I knew it wouldn't work out. I didn't feel I'd be very good company and I certainly didn't want to ruin their millennium celebration.

My appointment with Dr. Fass was the day prior to New Year's Eve. I was feeling extremely depressed. I almost felt sorry for my psychiatrist because she was always so positive and upbeat that it had to be difficult talking to negative, "broken men," such as myself day after day. I told her that I was really down and couldn't go on like this without any end in sight. I told her I felt worthless and had become a burden to everyone — not only to my family, but also to those at work. I had always been the one to take care of others; I always knew what to do, but now I had no confidence.

Dr. Fass then said, "Have you ever thought about suicide?"

"Yes, I have."

She then asked, "Do you have a plan?"

"Yes, I do." When I said that, Sandy looked at me shocked.

The psychiatrist then repeated herself, "You have a plan?"

"Yes," I responded.

"What is it?"

I broke down and cried as I told her I had thought about asphyxiating myself using carbon monoxide from my automobile exhaust system. It was the method used by Art Kart, a friend from high school who had committed suicide ten years earlier.

When the doctor asked why I would do such a thing, I told her it was because I could no longer care for my family.

"They'll get my life insurance."

"How much life insurance do you have?"

"A million dollars."

"A million dollars! Why so much?"

"I'm an insurance agent and I believe in my product. It has always been important to me to have the peace of mind knowing that I could take care of Sandy, Johnny, Debbie, and Jeff, even if I died prematurely."

Debbie kept a professional demeanor throughout my dialogue with Margo Fass. Dr. Fass focused on Sandy and said, "Because he perceives that he can no longer care for his family, he feels totally worthless and less of a man." Tears rolled down Sandy's face. The doctor then turned to Debbie and Sandy and said, "Do you want his life insurance money?" They both answered emphatically, "No." This response caused me to cry. Crying no longer bothered me. It seemed as if Dr. Fass's office had become the place that I could breakdown and cry. I actually looked forward to these weekly cries because I felt better afterwards. Dr. Fass then quizzed me as to my finances. I believe she was trying to show me the reality of my financial situation in order to convince me that I wasn't destined to live in a cardboard box on the street. My net worth was substantial, but I did not believe it was enough to support us for the rest of our lives without working. Sandy affirmed her belief that we could live on less, sell our home, do whatever it took to survive.

Dr. Fass continued discussing my "perceived" business and financial problems and then asked me if there was anything else that bothered me. I thought about it and tears began to swell in my eyes. Dr. Fass yelled, "Quickly, tell me what you are thinking about." I began to cry. When I regained my composure, I began to tell her about my sister and the way she had treated me since I was a little boy. I then told her how she once wished that I had died in Vietnam, and then I broke down again. Dr. Fass stared at me. "Who is this person you speak about?" "My sister," I said. The good doctor just stared and finally said, "What kind of person is she?" I also told her about the circumstances of my Mom's death and how badly I felt about having allowed Jean to change all my plans for Mom's care. I also felt guilty about not having stopped the angioplasty procedure. If I'd done that, she might still be alive.

She then went to her telephone and called Dr. Quirion at the Veterans Hospital in Bath. Dr. Q. had the day off so she called him at home. She explained who she was and that she thought my condition was critical. She feared for my safety and told him about my suicide plan. Dr. Q. apparently concurred with her based on our last visit. She then called the Canandaigua Veterans Hospital to see if a room was available. When she hung up the telephone, she turned to me and said, "I feel you should go into the hospital for your own safety." Although I knew the Canandaigua VA was a psychiatric facility, I said, "What kind of place is it?" When she told me, I said, "That's a snake pit." She did her best to convince me that it was a fine hospital.

I then, rather facetiously, said, "Will I be locked up?"

"Well, yes, the doors are locked, but that is for your own safety so you won't do harm to yourself."

I smiled at her and said, "Doctor Fass, this is the millennium. In twenty years when my grandchildren ask me where I was at the time of the millennium, I'm not going to tell them I spent it in a nuthouse."

I then got serious and said, "You asked me if I had a plan and I was honest when I said I had. However, I can honestly tell you that no matter how bad things get, I will not kill myself. I would never do that to my family. I love them too much. It also is against my religious beliefs."

Dr. Fass couldn't make me go, but she did give me a prescription that would allow me to be admitted to Canandaigua VA Hospital's psychiatric ward if I felt it was necessary. Prior to leaving her office she said, "I'm sorry these things happened to you." She was genuinely concerned and asked, "May I give you a hug?" We embraced and then Sandy and I departed for home.

We had made no plans for New Year's Eve. I couldn't wait to change into my nightclothes and relax in the safety of our home. I don't remember much about that evening. Perhaps Sandy prepared something special for dinner. I don't recall. At about 9 p.m. the doorbell rang and it was Ron and Donita Parmenter. They were good friends and lived close by. Ron was a Vietnam Vet and a successful automotive and tire entrepreneur. They had been out for dinner and stopped to visit. They both knew my problem and we felt comfortable talking with them. It made Sandy and my New Year's Eve much more enjoyable. As they prepared to leave, I gave Donita one of my now familiar hugs.

Well, I had survived the Millennium, but I wasn't getting any better. Life continued to be a struggle. Getting out of bed each morning and getting dressed for work was still an insurmountable task. My business could not have continued its smooth operation were it not for Emily, Anne, and Challiss. Every day was a struggle. I tried to walk whenever I could in order to build up endorphins.

Chapter 55

SEARCHING FOR ANSWERS

One day when I was really down, I sat in my car in the driveway. Ralph Diliberto, one of my clients, drove in behind me. It was quite obvious that I had a problem. I liked, respected, and trusted Ralph so I willingly explained my situation to him. He understood and had some insight into my problem. He had a book he wanted me to read, but said I was not in any condition to read it now. The biggest thing Ralph did for me that day was boost my self-esteem. After weeks of dwelling on all my negative attributes, Ralph began reminding me of my relationship with him and his family. They had moved here from New Jersey not knowing anyone. Most of them were self-employed craftsmen. I met them when I wrote their insurance programs and did what I could to help them and their businesses. I'd refer customers to them whenever I could. Actually, I did this for all my clients. I appreciated their business and was willing to help them any way I could, either on a personal or business level. It was nothing unusual, just who I was. I took it for granted until Ralph expressed his appreciation. His praise and his sincerity touched me deeply.

That evening I told Sandy, "Maybe I'm not such a bad person," and proceeded to tell her about my encounter with Ralph Diliberto. She did not seem surprised and said, "John, you don't realize it, but you've helped a lot of people over the years. You are a good person."

I did a great deal of reading during the month of January. I became a "student of depression." I learned as much about the disease as I could. I learned the difference between depression and anxiety. I analyzed the various medications and methods used to treat the ailment. I read articles by doctors, patients, mental health professionals, and families of patients. I'd also read inspirational books such as *Tuesdays with Morrie* and *Don't Sweat the Small Stuff.* I continued to read scripture, particularly those dealing with doubt, and those enforcing the message of God loving and caring for His flock. I continued to pray, asking that I be cured soon.

I still wasn't sure how long I could continue enduring this way of life. What previously seemed important to me, no longer mattered. The simple things in life were of real importance — such things as a good night's sleep, being able to wake up in the morning, enjoying a meal, or interacting with family and friends. Material objects were no longer important, they were just "things," "stuff" — they meant nothing. Peace of mind was the greatest gift one could possess. I truly believe a human being can handle physical illness better than mental illness. If a person has a rational, functioning brain, he or she can handle anything; without it, they are helpless. I also realize how important people are, not just family or friends, but also caring, empathetic strangers.

Dr. Fass suggested I take a vacation, but my perception was that I could not afford a vacation. Besides, how could Sandy or I enjoy ourselves in my present state of mind. I surely would not subject our friends in Florida or Arizona to having to "put up" with me.

Chapter 56

LISTENING AND FEELING

During February, Sandy continued to force me out of bed each morning and push me out the door. My three wonderful employees Anne, Emily and Challiss were extremely understanding and empathetic. They worked hard covering for me and kept the office operating smoothly. I will always be indebted, appreciative, and grateful to them. They were more than friends or co-workers — they were angels!

I had grown to hate my military service. I was once proud of having served my country, but now I realized how much pain the aftermath of the war had brought not only me, but also my family. I was once preoccupied with Vietnam, but now I couldn't stand the word, let alone read about it or watch a movie or TV show about it. I disliked John Wayne. His name wasn't even John, it was Marion. More than that, he never served a day in the military, yet he made a fortune glorifying war in his movies. An entire generation of boys like myself grew up "gung ho" on war because of John Wayne. After he filmed the movie *Green Berets*, the recruiters' phones were ringing off their hooks. I can only wonder how many young men were injured or died indirectly due to his war-glorifying movies.

Five months had passed and I still had not returned to my marital bed. I still dumped large doses of medications down my throat each morning and continued to take more pills at night in order to sleep. I was forcing myself to interact more. I hadn't spoken to my friend Al Bulkley in months. One day I sent him an e-mail and he wrote back. Al knew something about depression and purposely avoided contact with me. He knew that when I felt like talking I would. He interpreted my e-mail as a good sign — it meant I wanted to join the human race again. It was the first positive sign in a long time.

I began to listen to what others had to say — I mean truly listen. I kept my mouth shut and listened to what others had to say. I discovered that I wasn't the smartest guy in the world and that other people had good ideas and solid advice. My wife was a smart woman, yet I never took her advice because I thought I knew more than she did. I was wrong, and I overlooked a valuable asset all these years. Since I was so bullheaded about the way I did things, she finally quit making suggestions. Some of my "attitude" was a result of my PTSD. I had been so dependent upon myself for survival that I no longer trusted others.

Along with learning to listen, I began to "feel." I became so much more compassionate. There were situations that I had seen in the past, but never felt. I could see tragedy and hardship, but I never truly felt it. A couple in my church had two disabled sons as a result of a genetic disorder. One of the boys had recently died. I had seen the parents with their sons in church for many years. I thought how sad the situation was but never felt their pain. I now did. I realized that everyone had a "cross to bear." I admired these parents for their love, caring, perseverance, and faith in God.

Each day I would force myself to interact more at work. Getting out to see the people was the aspect of the business I'd always enjoyed most. This had always been my strong point, but the past few years I resigned myself to the office. I primarily handled the problem cases or customers that were upset, leaving me to deal with people at their worst. The more clients I visited, the more I would learn about life. I visited Darlene. She and her husband had been clients of our agency for many years. After discussing her homeowners insurance, she expressed an interest in some life insurance. As I departed her home, I thought what a beautiful woman she was. Her life seemed perfect.

The following day I called her with a life insurance quote. I had assumed she was in perfect health until she surprised me with the news that she suffered from MS. "Darlene, you show no apparent symptoms of MS," I said. "I'm fine in the house, but I need a cane to help me walk any distance," she replied. The more people I saw, the better I listened, the more compassionate I became, and the more I realized that we all have problems; no matter how perfect things looked on the outside, no one's life was perfect. We all had situations we had to deal with that are beyond our control. Father Austin was right when he told me that God was the one in control.

I would walk each evening trying to stimulate endorphins. I even began to lift weights with Ralph Diliberto at his furniture restoration shop. I would do anything to help myself get well. I wasn't particularly motivated about pumping iron, but I derived great benefits from talking with Ralph. He was a hard working, straight talking man that I respected. He also had a thorough knowledge of the Bible and was helpful in answering many of my spiritual questions. I would always leave his furniture restoration shop feeling much better. I was still taking large doses of anti-depressants and seeing Dr. Fass, but I felt as if I was experiencing moments of normalcy.

Chapter 57

REBIRTH

One day I came home from work actually feeling happy for the first time in a long, long time. When I entered the kitchen, I could tell by the look on Sandy's face that there was something wrong. I could tell she was upset, but I pressed her to tell me what was wrong. She finally told me that Jeff called her.

"Yes. Is there a problem," I asked.

"Jeff can no longer live a lie, John. He wants us to know he is gay."

"No. No. No," I cried. How much more can I take? I walked to the crucifix hanging in our hall. I screamed, "God, why are you doing this to me?" I then sobbed and fell to my knees. As I looked up at that crucifix, I heartbreakingly sobbed, "God, you've given me more than I can handle. I can't take anymore. Please Lord take this from me." Within seconds, I felt a calming peace come over me. I can honestly say that at that moment I was touched by the hand of God and changed forever.

I could feel the burden of these past months being lifted from me. I got off my knees, walked into the kitchen, and picked up the telephone. "Jeff, this is Dad. Mom told me what you told her. You are my son and I love you unconditionally."

249

John and son Jeff

The days that followed were days of reflection. They were not easy. I was not concerned about what people would say. I was concerned about my son's life and felt a certain amount of guilt. Not guilt about his sexuality, because I knew enough about the subject to know that one doesn't choose his or her sexuality. Whether we are heterosexual, bisexual, or homosexual is determined the moment of conception, no different than the color of one's eyes or hair.

I felt guilty for bringing him into a world that could be cruel and insensitive. I loved my children and worked and sacrificed so that their lives could be good. I then remembered Father Austin's words about my not being in control. God was in control. He was right. I had many challenges in life and had always been able to meet those challenges. Whatever was broken, I could fix. Whatever my mission was, I would accomplish it. Now I was faced with something I couldn't fix, but, with the grace of God, I would not let it defeat my family and me.

Sandy and I had an answer to the question we asked ourselves so often these past few months. We now knew why I had gone through this depression, why I had experienced the "Dark Night of the Soul." I now knew for myself what Jeff had experienced when he suffered with depression. No matter what Jeff was or wasn't, it couldn't be as bad as seeing him depressed. No parent wants to see the child that they love unable to function, not caring whether they live or die. Sandy said, "John, you could not have handled Jeff's announcement six months ago. You are now so much more compassionate and understanding."

As for Jeff, he felt like a huge boulder had been lifted from his shoulders. He knew since he was two years old that he was "different," but didn't know how or why. We now understand how difficult his childhood must have been. Children can be cruel, and I'm sure Jeff was on the receiving end of that cruelty. Yet he never complained or hated anyone. He was so forgiving of those who had treated him badly. He had always befriended others. It never mattered if a person was fat or thin, pretty or unattractive, rich or poor, smart or a poor academic. He was always honest and real, not a phony.

Sandy and I learned as much as we could about gays and lesbians by reading extensively. We felt we should see a counselor and were referred to Dr. Linda Mack, a clinical psychologist in Ithaca, New York. After our first session, Linda asked, "How long have you known about your son?" We said, "Five weeks." "Five weeks! I know parents who have known five years and don't handle it as well as you have. Jeff is lucky to have parents like you." I liked Linda, but took exception to her comment. "Linda, why is Jeff any luckier to have us as parents than we are to have him for a son? For us, nothing has changed; he is still the same kind, loving kid he always was. He never caused us any huge problems and has always been so considerate of others." Linda understood, but added that this isn't always the case. Many parents throw their kids out, which is why so many turn to drugs or commit suicide. Sandy and I couldn't for a moment feel this way. If anything, it made us determined to be more loving and supportive of our son.

I was extremely proud of my family. The way they handled this situation spoke volumes about their character. Sandy was the loving mother she had always been. Tambi, my daughter-in-law, was one of the first to know. She and Jeff are both artists and were very close. Tambi is accepting of others and did not see Jeff's sexuality as an issue. When I asked Debbie for her reaction, she turned the psychological chairs on me by asking me how I felt about it. She finally responded that she thought it was wonderful that Jeff could be who he is and not have to live a lie. I am most proud of the way Johnny responded. Weeks had passed and Jeff never told his older brother. One day, Johnny, who is 6' and 230 pounds, walked up to his little brother, put his arm around him and said, "Jeff, don't agonize about telling me. I already know. You're my brother and I love you."

When Johnny and I had a chance to discuss things alone, I said, "Why Jeff? It was Jeff that needed eyeglasses. It was Jeff that needed dental braces. Why did he have to be gay?" "Dad," John said, "It had to be Jeff." "Why," I asked puzzled. "Because I'm not strong enough to be gay. Jeff is the only one that is mentally and spiritually strong enough. He's been a bullhead since he was a baby and, Dad, you are the last person I'd want to have to tell something like that to!" His answer was profound but true.

We continued seeing the counselor several more times. Her insight was helpful. She gave us books to read and referred us to PFLAG (Parents and Friends of Lesbians and Gays). A local physician with his wife had formed the local chapter after learning their son was gay. After our fourth or fifth session, Linda asked what we wanted from her. We just wanted some feedback as to how we were handling this. She said that she couldn't believe how well we were dealing with all of this and that we were doing everything right. As a matter of fact, she asked me the reason for it. I told her the truth. God was helping us. By now, prayer had become part of my daily routine. I needed it to start my day and I needed it to end my day. Each afternoon I would also get down on my knees to thank God for his blessings and ask him to help me with all aspects of my life. I'm not a preacher, I never have been, and probably never will be, but when people ask me how I got through the severe depression and all the other obstacles, I have to tell them the truth: "God helped me."

Chapter 58

THE RESURRECTION

In early spring, Chuck and Faith Ciprich invited us to ride to Florida with them. I was still depressed and having sleep problems, but I felt a little better so we agreed to go. Chuck had arranged for me to drive a used car back for a local automobile dealer. Sandy and I stayed with Aunt Rose and Uncle Steve and also visited her folks in Myrtle Beach. Her folks wintered there for many years, but this was the first time we visited them.

When we returned from our vacation, I proceeded to tell our friends about Jeff. I did not want them to hear it via rumors, and I didn't want them to feel uncomfortable around us. One at a time, I saw each of them over a period of several weeks. It was something I chose to do. Our friends were all understanding and accepting. Their comments were all the same, "We love Jeff; he's a great kid, and nothing has changed." I was disappointed with the responses from my brother Bob and from my close friend Bev. Both are fundamentalist Christians. In my opinion, they don't accept those who are different. This upset me until Jeff spoke to me, "Dad, people like myself ask that others be accepting of us as being different. As such, we too should accept those that think differently than us." He asked me not to be angry with my brother or Bev.

As the days went by and the weather changed from frosty mornings to sunny days, I too began to feel better. I began to regain my appetite. One day I wound my clocks and started them. Sandy later told me that this was her first glimmer of hope that my Dark Journey was coming to an end. Then one morning she heard me singing in the shower and, for the first time in months, allowed herself to think that perhaps this hellish nightmare was ending.

I pushed myself to get out and contact my clients either in person, on the phone, or by mail. I had to do my best to make the business not only work, but also grow. I did not hide my depression, the Post-Traumatic Stress or Jeff's revelation. It was therapeutic for me to talk about it. I was not the least bit embarrassed by any of it. As a matter of fact, by sharing my experiences with others, I was getting back more than I was giving. Unlike many people who would hide family "secrets," I was strong enough to share my weaknesses. After all, all people have problems, whether they admit it or not.

Several prominent, and not so prominent, members of our community confided to me that they too had experienced bouts of depression. Most had not been as severe as mine, but, nonetheless, they had suffered. Likewise, there were very few families that didn't have someone in their family or a close friend who was gay or lesbian. People were much more accepting than they were a generation ago. It was still painful to hear people unknowingly make jokes. I'm sure I may have been guilty of doing the same in the past. I now know it was wrong and that people who show their intolerance to any group that is "different" are only publicly displaying their lack of maturity, lack of compassion, and ignorance. Life can be tough and we, as God's children, were meant to accept one another's differences, and help one another get through our journey in life.

I recall driving through Horseheads, N.Y. when I spotted a poorly dressed, unshaven man shuffling near Route 86. I stopped the car and watched him. In the past, I would have probably driven by thinking, "What a bum, get a job." But now I realized this was someone's husband, father, son, or brother. He possibly suffered from a mental illness. "There, but for the grace of God, go I," I thought. I said a prayer for the man before I drove off.

The following day, I came to work and the staff acted sullen. When I asked what was wrong, they showed me the morning newspaper. The post office contract had been awarded to the out of town developer. It was an obvious injustice; it was backroom politics at work. They didn't even call or write to me. I had to learn about it from the newspaper. Sandy walked in about then and the girls filled her in on the latest news. I could hear them discussing it. They were upset and concerned. Upset because Sandy and I had not been treated fairly, and concerned that this would throw me back into that deep dark pit. When I approached them, they said, "You don't look very upset by all this." I replied, "I'm not. I've had four good days and hopefully tomorrow I'll have five. Apparently, God doesn't want us to own a post office. Building a post office would have come with a price tag, perhaps additional stress. For whatever reason, we weren't meant to have it."

If I had a choice of owning a post office or being free of depression, it would be no choice. Waking up each day feeling good, having a loving wife and family, caring friends, being able to fall asleep at night, enjoying food, being free of anxiety, and having a personal relationship with God is what is truly important.

Chapter 59

THE ASCENDANCE OF
SPIRITUAL PURPOSE

As I end this book, I close another chapter in my life; almost three years have passed. I continue to take medications because of my fear of ever falling into that depressed state of mind. Sandy and I spend more quality time with one another, our children, and our close friends. I have divorced myself from various clubs and boards although I do try to assist on a few select worthy causes throughout the year. My business experienced several changes that caused me some anxiety. Our agency now has "new blood" and we are now stronger than before. We are growing. I enjoy coming to work. I give my staff as many days off and long weekends as I can. I want them to enjoy both their work and their families.

My son Johnny and Tambi had a beautiful wedding in Hopetown, Bahamas. Our friends and family stayed there for a week. Debbie was a bridesmaid and Johnny chose Jeff to be his best man. Debbie has changed her career path from education to homeopathic medicine. Jeff and his partner Stan live with us as Jeff has returned to college and Stan completes his teaching degree. Johnny has opened his own insurance agency in Bath, N.Y. and is doing well.

About a year into writing this book, I surprised Sandy with a formal renewal of our wedding vows. Our marriage is now stronger than ever. We try to keep our lives simple. We value our friendships and try to help others as much as we can. The pond we started is finished and we hope to build our vacation home this spring. Sandy refers to it as "Golden Pond," but I tell her I'm a long way from retiring — I have too much to do. We look forward to my Army reunions and sharing stories with other members of the 4th Battalion 9th Infantry "Manchus." We take life a day at a time, count our blessings, and put our faith in God. I am again proud to have served in the defense of Freedom and against the spread of tyranny.

More than thirty-five years have passed since the Vietnam War and the turbulent '60s. Since the era following Desert Storm, this country has done a complete turn around in its perception of the Vietnam Veteran. As the boys of the '60s approach middle age, one thing is clear. The Vietnam Veteran is not a drug crazed, homeless misfit as portrayed by the media for so many years.

History has shown that the majority of our Vietnam Veterans returned home having served their country well. They returned to college campuses or to careers. Most of them married and raised families. They are your doctors, policemen, attorneys, firemen, teachers and business owners. You will find them serving on school boards, municipal boards, in state and federal government.

It is my personal observation that the Vietnam Vets are more comfortable with their decision than are the draft dodgers and deserters.

It is quite clear that the liberal "intellectuals" were not as much concerned with the truth about the war as they were about pushing their own agendas. The deceitful propaganda and half-truths spread by the left wing enemy within, gave them their justification. They were concerned with saving their own skin.

We Vietnam Vets had the same concerns. We certainly were not pro war. We were afraid of dying or being maimed. The difference between "us" and "them" was our intestinal fortitude and our value system. We instinctively put our country before ourselves, trusting in its worthy purposes.

Ho Chi Min said that he would defeat us from within and the liberal "intellectuals" were his tools. They had a captive audience for a generation. They taught that the anti-war movement was what was right. Some professors went so far as to teach that it took more courage to protest against the government, burn your draft card, and desecrate the American flag than it did to fight a fierce enemy under harsh conditions on foreign soil. They got away with this for awhile, but in the past few years our young people began to ask questions. Our children wanted to hear the other side of the story and were hungry to learn all they could. Vietnam Veterans began to come forward to tell their story. They volunteered to speak to high school and college classes. Vietnam Veteran educators offered classes on the Vietnam War. In one local college, the course was in such demand that those students who applied to take the course as freshman would finally get into the course as seniors.

As these youngsters heard the other side of the story, they confronted their parents, teachers, and other liberal "intellectuals." The responses were amazing. They ranged from embarrassment, to apologies, to excuses such as "we were young" or "it was a long time ago." A book could be written about these responses.

Most of those who ran to Canada, Sweden, and other safe havens scurried back to the good old U.S.A. with their tails between their legs as soon as Jimmy Carter allowed it. I see these men each day in my own community; and every community has them. They are conspicuously absent at Veterans Day or Memorial Day ceremonies.

It is now clear that Vietnam was the essential last war necessary to defeat Communist plans for World conquest and domination. History will acknowledge this.

The determination of the Free World in both Korea and Vietnam against deceitful and vicious tyranny defeated their rapid take over of all of South East Asia. It held them at bay and bled their resources long enough for other world developments to cause the collapse of that enslaving tyranny in the very heart of its beginnings. I firmly believe that if we had not fought in Vietnam, this collapse would not have occurred.

Perhaps the greatest lesson of Vietnam is not the failure of government to adequately support and direct the battle there, nor is it the killings that took place.

The greatest lesson may be that when leaders of our nation do not fully define and support justified decisions to defend moral principals, our soldiers feel abandoned by their country and their god. The soldiers thus become separated from both a legitimate purpose and a righteous soul. The struggle to regain our soul is what PTSD is all about. Vietnam Veterans must make that journey.

Now that I have resolved within myself, both the justified purposes and the moral rightness of the struggle of a free people against the threatening spread of evil tyranny in Vietnam, I can stand tall and proud of my service to my country and to the cause of freedom.

EPILOGUE

For three and a half years following my bout with severe depression I not only recovered, but also became physically stronger, spiritually wiser, and more compassionate. My business experienced many difficult changes, but also grew and became stronger.

I was doing so well that I decided to stop taking my medication and in June 2003 I relapsed into serious depression. This time I knew what to expect and learned to compensate. Nonetheless, it was horrible and it hurt. I began to seriously study depression in an effort to prevent it from ever striking me again. I took a fifteen-week self-study course and an eight-week cognitive therapy class at the Veterans Hospital. I got back on my medication and also turned to a homeopathic remedy. It took most of the summer to recover, and robbed Sandy and me of the usual summer activities.

Sandy also became depressed. She felt as if she had "no more to give." Sandy ran between me and her parents, who were in the hospital and could no longer function independently. By summer's end the depression was gone and we were able to attend my Army reunion in Florida, and I was able to teach the fall semester at the local college.

This relapse, as painful as it was, brought blessings. It strengthened relationships, and instilled my desire to help others. Sandy and I began to pray together each day, something we had never done. We also made it our goal to further simplify our lives, to rid ourselves of "stuff," to enjoy our family and friends more, to have fun, and to enjoy nature.

We feel blessed in so many ways.

___Thirteen Things I Have Learned from Experiencing the Dark Night of the Soul___

1. We <u>are not</u> in control, God is.
2. God comes first in our lives. Before family. Before jobs. Without Him, we cannot handle these other aspects of our lives.
3. Next to our relationship with God, our relationship with our spouse and children is most important and essential for a happy life.
4. Friends, and even strangers, can be more supportive, caring, and concerned than relatives.
5. Relatives and family are not the same.
6. Life can be rough. We must help one another over the rough spots.
7. Sometimes it's easier to go around the mountain than over it.
8. We must learn to simplify our lives. Get rid of "stuff." Do not accumulate "stuff." Take time each morning to meditate and pray.
9. Mental illness is more disabling than physical illness. If one has a rational, functioning mind, he or she can handle anything.
10. "Good Days" should not be taken for granted. They should be embellished and cherished.
11. When a human being is reduced to nothing, he or she will be molded into a stronger more compassionate person.
12. God <u>demands</u> that we be accepting and tolerant of those who are different than us. We should not judge people by their appearance, their ethnic background, their religion, the color of their skin, or their sexual orientation. To do so is a serious offense against God.
13. We can, and should, forgive those that have hurt us, but we do not have to go back for more. We must also learn to forgive ourselves.

About the Author

John Senka grew up in Arkport, the son of the late Joseph and Julia Katsur. He graduated from Arkport Central School in 1965 and attended Alfred State College.

In 1967, John volunteered for the draft. He completed Basic Training at Fort Dix, N.J. and received advanced infantry and jungle training at Ft. Jackson, S.C., where he later served as Drill Sgt.

In the fall of 1968, John was sent to the Army 25th Infantry Division as a combat infantryman in Vietnam. During a Christmas Truce, the North Vietnamese Army attacked his unit at a place called Mole City, near the Cambodian Border. It was a suicide mission for the NVA — they had their grave markers strapped to their backs. John was severely wounded in this battle. As a last resort, his unit called in artillery fire on their own base camp.

John received numerous decorations, including the Bronze Star, Purple Heart, Vietnam Campaign Medal, Vietnam Service Medal, Presidential Unit Citation, Army Commendation for Valor, N.Y. State Conspicuous Service Cross, and the Combat Infantryman's Badge.

He has been married to his wife, Sandy, for almost thirty-five years and is the father of a daughter and two sons. He lives in Montour Falls where he owns an independent insurance agency.

I think former Marine Sgt. Jack Howe expressed the sentiments of most Vietnam Veterans in his speech at the "Moving Wall":

"It didn't seem to be such a great honor at the time, but looking back on it, I realize now what a privilege it was to be given the opportunity to engage the enemies of our country on the field of battle; a privilege granted to relatively few men in this country."

Moving Vietnam memorial comes to Arkport

By JEFFERY SMITH
Staff writer

ARKPORT — Families, friends and people who served beside the many veterans who lost their lives in the Vietnam conflict can honor the fallen soldiers this weekend as a portable replica of the Vietnam Memorial Wall will be on display at the Arkport American Legion.

The wall will be open to the public beginning at 10 a.m. today, said Randy Baker, Legion member.

"This is a special day for the family members of the all the soldiers who lost their lives for our country," said Doug Baker, commander of the Arkport American Legion Post, "and for the soldiers who served along side of these men and women."

The drive to bring the wall to Arkport was initiated by Danny Hartwell and John Senka. The two were boyhood friends of Fredrick Donald Kemp, an Arkport native who lost his life in the war "All three of them served in the war," said Doug Baker, "but Freddy never returned."

In the memory of their lost friends, the two decided to bring the wall to the village of Arkport.

Randy Baker said this is a great way to honor all the men and women who were killed in the war between 1959 and 1975.

"It's a great honor for us as a community to have the wall here," he said. "It's a piece of history and a way to remember and honor those who gave their lives."

See WALL, Page 2A

THE LEADER/BILL WELLER

The reflection of the U.S. flag shines Thursday in the Vietnam Memorial Wall set up at the American Legion in Arkport.

Hornell Evening Tribune

Arkport natives honor Vietnam buddy

Three childhood pals served in the war, but one didn't return home

The traveling replica of the Vietnam Memorial Wall in Washington D.C. arrives in Arkport today as two Vietnam vets honor a boyhood buddy who died in that war 30 years ago.

The wall will be open to the public 24 hours a day until Sunday at 3 p.m.

Arkport is about five miles north of Hornell on Route 36.

Known as the "healing wall," the wall's visit to Arkport was sparked by John Senka of Odessa and Dan Hartwell of Arkport.

Dan, John and Marine Lance Cpl. Freddy Kemp were Arkport natives who shared boyhood dreams in that town of about 700.

All three served in Vietnam. Army infantrymen Dan and John came back. Freddy didn't.

The traveling wall's appearance is to honor Freddy on the 30th anniversary of his death. Arkport American Legion Post 1248 is sponsoring the wall, paying the $,000 fee and the premium on a liability insurance policy.

The renovated Arkport Junior baseball field, named for Freddy, will also be re-dedicated. Ceremonies take place at 1 p.m. Saturday.

The Marine Corps Honor Guard will be there from Rochester and the National Guard will stand sentry at the wall.

John Senka nearly died in Vietnam. He was only 20 when he volunteered for the draft and was assigned to the 25th Infantry Division's Charlie Company, 4th Battalion, 9th Infantry, known as the Manchus.

His outfit was ordered to build a fire support base on the Cambodian border. Later, John learned that the base was set up to draw the enemy.

It worked.

On Dec. 22, 1968, the base was overrun by a 1,500 North Vietnamese Army regulars on a suicide mission.

Provided

John Senka of Odessa, right, and Dan Hartwell of Arkport were boyhood friends in Arkport. Here, they are pictured in Vietnam during the late 1960s. They started a movement that led to a visit by the Vietnam Memorial Wall replica to Arkport this weekend.

The base was called Mole City because of the trenches and bunkers John's unit dug. A book, "Suicide Charlie," by Norman Russell, tells the story.

John was one of four in a bunker and the only survivor. He was badly wounded, but he remembered one soldier who piled some bodies on top of him to hide the fact that he was alive.

John was hospitalized with abdomen, leg and ear injuries for six months.

Unlike other Vietnam vets, he found only compassion and respect when he came home. "Nobody spit on me in Arkport," he said.

He was asked to speak at a local school at that time but couldn't.

That has changed. John has healed some over the last 30 years during which he twice visited the Vietnam Wall in Washington.

He spoke at Arkport services last Memorial Day and is one of three guest speakers at Saturday's ceremony.

He figures he needs to show his appreciation to Arkport for the way he was treated when he came home from war.

Today, John, 51, owns a successful insurance agency in Odessa. He's married to the former Sandy Nikl of Endwell, N.Y., and they have three children.

Elmira Star Gazette

Thank you for coming out to honor our war dead and our living Veterans. I am proud to be part of the Village of Watkins Glen's 2001 Memorial Day Ceremonies. I have many fond memories of growing up in a small rural village similar to Watkins Glen and would like to recall my earliest memories of Memorial Days, as a young boy in the early 1950s.

As a child in the 1950s, I don't think we youngsters understood that World War II had only been over a few years or that a war was raging in Korea. I can still remember my neighbor calling cadence with a .45 pistol strapped to his side. While all of the Village Veterans marched, Memorial Day parades excited the young people. As we grew older, we would decorate our bikes and participate in the parade. We often stood silently in the cemetery in awe of the 21-gun salute. I remember the same gray-haired lady placing a wreath on a grave each year. That was the first time I learned the meaning of a Gold Star Mother. The lady's name was Mrs. Wellington. Her son had been killed in World War II.

As Boy Scouts, we took an active part in Memorial Day events. During that era, patriotism was alive and well in villages such as Watkins Glen. Most of us growing up in the 1950s had a love for our great country and respect for our flag. So it was not surprising that when, in the mid 1960s, the United States got involved in Vietnam, many of the young men and women in villages such as Watkins Glen answered their country's call – people like Gary Gascon, Danny Love, Alvin Merrich, Bob Pastore, Bob Stanko, Robert Voorheis, and Virginia Harrington, whose names appear on the memorial of this Courthouse lawn. They did not question their politicians' motives or choose their war. They did not run off to Canada, Sweden, or some other safe haven. They felt it was their duty to serve. They felt the same as their fathers did in World War II or those that served in Korea before them. In small villages, a disproportionately large number of men and women served in the military. Many of you here today, standing before me, have served in World War II, Korea, Vietnam, or Desert Storm; and you should be proud of your military service. Some of you like myself were sent to Vietnam and remember the intense heat, mud, and monsoons. We never forget the fear we felt the first time a bullet "cracked" over our head, a mortar round sent shrapnel in our direction, or a booby trap exploded in the jungle. Nor do we forget the loneliness from being away from home or the sadness we felt the first time one of our buddies died.

Some of you, like myself, shed your blood in places such as Cu Chi, Tay Ninh, Normandy, Anzio Beach, Iwo Jima, Pork Chop Hill, or the Chosin Reservoir. To this day we all feel the pain of the loss of our comrades. Not a day goes by that I don't think of Hank Maul, a Mormon from Wyoming who looked forward to returning to his job as a hunting guide; Justin Anderson, a Swede from Chicago who had just earned a masters degree; Phil Glen, a farm boy from Arkansas who wanted to become a police officer; Malcolm True, a young father from Cocoa Beach, Florida who yearned to return to his wife and son; Jay Schmid, a twenty-six-year old man from New Jersey who had recently inherited a home in Germany and was the heir to the Schmid family business; or Freddy Kemp, my childhood friend who had the potential of becoming a Major League baseball player. All six were killed in 1968 in Vietnam. Four of them were in my bunker.

We Americans, standing here today, owe an enormous debt of gratitude to our World War II Veterans — they truly were the Greatest Generation and deserve a fitting memorial while they are still here to see it; to our Korean War Veterans who fought a forgotten war; and the 58,000 plus men and eight women who died in Vietnam. I, for one, will never forget their sacrifices. They remain in my heart and prayers today and every day. I am certain that all who died for freedom are in Heaven with our Creator.

Let us also not forget the Vietnam Veterans who came home and weren't given much of a welcome. Some Americans blamed the war on the warrior. It has been a difficult time for many of us. Veterans are still dying today from the effects of Agent Orange, drugs, alcohol, loneliness, and despair. Many are disabled from physical, as well as psychological, injuries. So please remember them in your prayers.

The greatest love one can have is to lay down one's life for their brothers and sisters. And that's exactly what all men and women killed in all of our wars did for us so that we might enjoy our freedom today. Let us always honor them in our hearts.

I pray for an outbreak of peace all over this world. I pray that the hearts of all world leaders be open so that they may embrace the risks involved in making peace rather than making war…

I'd like to close with a poem inspired by a 1963 letter written by John Keith in the jungles of Vietnam:

"Who Will Bury Me"

We buried another today mother, that's the third one on this cold
    dark trail.
Each night I close my eyes mother, my nightmares send me to
    hell.
But even my dreams are nothing compared to the reality here.
I have to stop writing now mother, we're on the move again.
Say a prayer mother, say a prayer for me and my friends. It's
    been three days mother.
Three days of mud and rain.
Two more bodies lay to rest in this foreign land we're in.
But only 150 days left mother, till I come home again.
Home, I don't know how home will be.
I don't know how things will look without blood on every tree.
There are only five of us left now mother, and miles away from
    anywhere.
I have to go now mother, but please don't forget my prayer.
Well mother, there are just two of us now, and Tom has been hit
    pretty bad.
The other three left us just yesterday.
But I'm too cold, wet, and afraid to be sad.
We buried them in the dead of night.
Just a few words muttered on the sight.

I'm afraid now mother, you'll never get to read these last words I
     write.
But don't shed a tear for me mother, it was my choice to fight.
I'll die knowing my death is the price of your freedom.
Got to go now mother, Tom needs my help. My hands are almost
     too cold to write now mother, but they are the only things
     I had to dig Tom's grave.
If I ever make it back mother, what will they say?
Call me a hero or say that I'm brave?
But what will they say of the ones that lie still?
Their praises will go unheard by their deafened ears.
I'm ready now mother, ready for what the Lord has prepared for
     me.
My only fear now mother, is "who will bury me?"

Thank you and may God bless America.

Arkport GI Hurt In Vietnam Action

ARKPORT—Sp. 4 John Senka, son of Mr. and Mrs. Joseph Katsur of 29 Main St., Arkport, was wounded in action on Dec. 22 in Vietnam.

Senka suffered fragmentation wounds of both legs and the abdomen. One leg was broken when six enemy grenades entered the bunker which he occupied, according to a report received by his family.

The soldier was a member of the 4th Battalion, 9th Infantry Regiment (Manchus) of the 25th Division. He received his wounds one mile from the Cambodian border during a ground assault by the Viet Cong, Katsur said.

Senka was treated at a Vietnam hospital and then evacuated to the 106th General Hospital in Japan for further treatment. He is expected to return to the United States in about three weeks. The soldier has been in Vietnam since October.

Rochester Times Union

Bronze Star Is Awarded Arkport Man

ARKPORT — The Bronze Star Medal has been awarded to Spec. 4 John T. Senka, son of Mr. and Mrs. Joseph P. Katsur of RD 1, Arkport, for "meritorious achievement in ground operations against hostile forces in the Republic of Vietnam," it was learned recently.

Senka, receiving the nation's fourth highest award, also holds the Army Commendation for Heroism, the Purple Heart, the Vietnam Service Medal, the Vietnam Campaign Medal, National Defense and the Combat Infantry Badge.

The citation was given by the direction of the President of the United States.

Hornell Evening Tribune

GENERAL ORDERS
NUMBER   1415

10 February 1969

AWARD OF THE ARMY COMMENDATION MEDAL FOR HEROISM

1. TC 320. The following AWARD is announced.

SENKA, JOHN T. US52967965 (SSAN: 066-38-8245) SP4
Co C, 4th Bn, 9th Inf, 25th Inf Div
Awarded: Army Commendation Medal with "V" Device
Date action: 22 December 1968
Theater: Republic of Vietnam
Reason: For heroism in connection with military operations against a
hostile force: Specialist Senka distinguished himself by heroic
actions on 22 December 1968, while serving with Company C, 4th
Battalion, 9th Infantry in the Republic of Vietnam. While
established in their patrol base, Company C came under a fierce
attack by a numerically superior enemy force. With complete
disregard for his own safety, Specialist Senka remained at his
post as the intensity of the battle grew and the defense was
breached by the aggressors. Exposed to enemy fire, he engaged
the insurgents as they moved towards friendly bunker areas.
His valorous actions contributed immeasurably to the defeating
of the enemy and the success of the mission. Specialist Senka's
personal bravery, aggressiveness, and devotion to duty are in
keeping with the highest traditions of the military service
and reflect great credit upon himself, his unit, the 25th
Infantry Division, and the United States Army.
Authority: By the direction of the Secretary of the Army under the
provisions of AR 672-5-1, and USARV Reg 672-1.

FOR THE COMMANDER:

OFFICIAL:

T. EDWARDS
CW2, USA
Asst AG

ROBERT L. FAIR
Colonel, GS
Chief of Staff

DISTRIBUTION:
D (Modified) Plus
3-CO, 1st Bde, 25th Inf Div
2-CO, 4th Bn, 9th Inf
10-Act Br
4-Indiv conc
1-Enl Pers Br
1-Div CSM

SPECIAL DISTRIBUTION:
1-AGPERSCEN ATTN: AGPE-F
Fort Benjamin Harrison
Indiana 46216

Recovering From Wounds In Japan

ARKPORT — Army Specialist Four John Senka, 21, son of Mr. and Mrs. Joseph Katsur, Arkport RFD 1, is recuperating in Japan from wounds received in Vietnam Dec. 22, his parents recently learned.

A member of the Fourth Battalion, Ninth Infantry, Twenty-fifth Division. Senka suffered grenade fragmentation wounds in a ground assault by Viet Cong near the Cambodian border in the Saigon district.

SENKA UNDERWENT surgery in an Army hospital in Vietnam for fragmentation wounds of the abdomen and both legs and a broken leg. He was evacuated to the 106th General Hospital in Japan, where he had a second operation.

His parents expect his return to the United States in about three weeks.

Senka had been in Vietnam about two months before he was injured.

Is Awarded Valor Medal

ARKPORT — Sp. 4 John T. Senka, son of Mr. and Mrs. Joseph Katsur of Arkport RFD 1, was recently awarded the Army Commendation Medal with Valor for heroism in Vietnam and the Purple Heart.

The Army noted that Senka, in connection with military operations against a hostile force, distinguished himself by heroic actions on December 22, 1968, in Vietnam.

Senka's infantry company came under attack by a large enemy force. The commendation went on to say that Senka, "with complete disregard for his own safety, remained at his post as the intensity of the battle grew and the defense was breached by the aggressors."

Wounded in the attack, Senka is recuperating from injuries at the U.S. Army Hospital in Ft. Devans, Mass.

Hornell Evening Tribune

MILITARY MAILBAG: U.S. Army Specialist Four John T. Senka has been awarded the Combat Infantry man badge for sustained combat against the enemy while stationed with the 25th Infantry Division's 9th Infantry in Vietnam. Spec. Senka, 21, is the son of Mr. and Mrs. Joseph P. Katsur of Arkport Road ... Seaman Douglas L. Kerr Jr. U.S. Navy, son

John Senka of Cohocton shows the "conspicuous service" award he received last month from Governor Rockefeller. The award was given because Senka received the Purple Heart and Bronze Star while serving in Vietnam. He received the award over three years after his discharge from the Army.

'Conspicuous Service' Award to Cohoctonite

COHOCTON — It was three years late in coming but John Senka of Cohocton finally received his award.

Senka, who received the Purple Heart and Bronze Star while serving in Vietnam, said the two awards means the automatic presentation of a third one, a certificate for "conspicuous service" awarded by Governor Rockefeller. Senka received the certificate last month, three and a half years after his discharge from the Army.

An insurance agent in Cohocton, Senka is a 1965 graduate of Arkport Central School. He is a business graduate of the State Agricultural and Technical College at Alfred and attended Rochester Business Institute. He is the son of Mr. and Mrs. Joseph Katsur of Arkport.

Senka, who is presently the president of the Cohocton Lion's Club, is married to the former Sandra Nikl of Binghamton. They have two children, Debbie, 2 and John, two months.

Hornell Evening Tribune

Mole City

Dearest Sandy,

Hi baby. How is everything? Hope all is well.

I guess you know by now that I was wounded. For awhile there I didn't think I'd ever see you again, but after over 6 hours of "HELL!" I came out in pretty good shape and I should have no physical handicaps, just a few scars. I got hit with at least 6 hand grenades, it's a miracle I came out so well. I'll tell you the whole story when I get home. I'm in Japan now. They took the fragmentation out of me in a VN hospital and they'll sew me back up here. I'll probably go into surgery in a day or 2, the doctor said if all goes well, I'll be home in 2 or 3 weeks. They'll send me to the closest Army hospital to my house, probably in N.Y. City, but I'll see if I can get transfered to Bath VA. Good news isn't it? I told you not to worry about me - hope my Mother took the news o.k. Well honey, I've got to rest, stop writing.

Love,
John

P.S. I shaved my moustache.
I want no reminders of
Viet Nam.

SANDRA NIKL

The engagement of Miss Sandra Nikl to John T. Senka has been announced by her parents, Mr. and Mrs. Louis H. Nikl of Endwell. Mr. Senka is the son of Mr. and Mrs. Joseph P. Katsur of Arkport.

The bride-elect is a 1965 graduate of Maine-Endwell Senior High School and attended State Agricultural and Technical College at Alfred. She is attending Binghamton School of Nursing, where she will graduate in February.

Mt. Senka, a 1965 graduate of Arkport Central School, attended Alfred Tech and graduated from Rochester Business Institute. He is serving with the U.S. Army.

Wedding plans are incomplete.

Hornell Evening Tribune

Sandy and John, wedding day

Sandy and John at
Insurance Convention, Rome, Italy

Sandy and John
Vacation at Puerto Rico

Wounded Body – Healing Spirit

Order Form

Use this form to order additional copies of
Wounded Body – Healing Spirit

Please Print:

Name _________________________________

Address _______________________________

City _____________________ **State** _________

Zip _________

Phone ( ) _____________________

_____ copies of book @ $23.95 each $ _______
Postage and handling $3.05 per book $ _______
NY residents add 8.25% tax $ _______
Total amount enclosed $ _______

<u>Make checks payable to John T. Senka</u>

Send to John T. Senka
P.O. Box 150 • Odessa, NY 14869